GREAT
BATH
IDEAS

WILEY

John Wiley & Sons, Inc.

GREAT BATH IDEAS

For general information about our other products and services, please contact our Customer Care Department within the United States at (800) 762-2974, outside the United States at (317) 572-3993 or fax (317) 572-4002.

Wiley also publishes its books in a variety of electronic formats. Some content that appears in print may not be available in electronic books. For more information about Wiley products, visit our web site at www.wiley.com.

ISBN 978-0-470-49041-9

Printed in the United States of America

10 9 8 7 6 5 4 3 2 1

TABLE OF CONTENTS

196

Bathrooms are the most personal and individual rooms in the house. Some of us (teenagers in particular) have been known to linger in them for hours, whether in front of a mirror or under a showerhead. To the rest of the family, such an expenditure of time may seem mysterious, but to the person using the bathroom, time stands still in a perfect cocoon of self-indulgence and introspection. Some of us have found the addition of wall-hung and floor magazine racks an inspired amenity in the bathroom, while others only scratch their heads at the idea that this space could supply two of the best reading areas in the home.

Bathrooms are where we go to get ready for a party. We clean up and apply our war paint, do our hair, and check the final beautiful package that is us. Bathrooms are where we go when we don't feel so well after the party; they supply us with the soothing deluge of a hot shower or the restorative splash of cool water. This room witnesses our triumphs and our failures. It keeps our secrets and prepares us for the more public areas of our lives. It is considered a necessity but can be the biggest luxury in the home. Bottom line: The way each of us uses this essential space is completely personal, private, and extremely idiosyncratic.

Of all the rooms in the home, bathrooms can generate the strongest territorial urges, straining otherwise harmonious relationships. For this reason, if space and budget allow, couples may choose their own personal vanities and toilet rooms off the main bathing area. Conversely, if space and budget allow, extra-large tubs and showers roomy enough for two can keep romance alive in a relationship.

New innovations in plumbing have been introduced to further reduce the potential for conflict in the "his and hers" turf wars of this space. I speak of the wonderful invention of the self-activated toilet seat. This product senses your approach and raises the lid, flushes when you leave, and, best of all, lowers the seat and lid upon completion. The ongoing debate about whether to leave the lid up or down can now end.

In a related trend, urinals have pushed aside the bidet as the new luxury novelty item. Don't expect these new fixtures to look utilitarian: Sculptors and high-end manufacturers have embraced designing and producing these cutting-edge vessels, and the results range from artistic to witty.

As technology advances, new and fun looks are turning up in a space that in past centuries was nothing more than a hole in the ground. LED lights are finding their way into all sorts of applications in today's bath. Tiles light up, urinals and sinks can change colors with the flick of a switch, and even mirrors now have lights hidden behind their silvery surfaces.

In the never-ending quest for healthful living, chromatherapy has been added to the experience of bathing. Some people feel that changing the color of the tub's water can affect your mood, so bathtubs are now available with a choice of LED colored lights. They change the color of the bath water, enhancing the therapeutic effect of a long hot soak.

If it used to be impossible for you to have a TV in the loo because of a lack of space, that problem has been solved by the new combination mirror-LCD TV units. Now you can catch up on any show while brushing your pearly whites.

Audio hasn't been left behind in this surge of technical wizardry; new, innovative tiles work like mini speakers, allowing the addition of music to the shower. Now the only thing to worry about is how off-key you may be when singing along.

It seems every year new inventions take us further and further into realizing our bathing fantasies. You'll see many of them in the pages that follow. (For more information on the products shown, check the Resources pages at the back of the book.) At the end of the day, what most people really want is a room that meets their basic needs—for me, that list would include that it be pretty, spacious, have two of everything, lots of storage, maybe a chair or dressing table; two showerheads would be good, oh, and a deep tub.

That's why I did this book—we all want a porcelain palace.

Betsy Speert

Bathroom Trends

1

It's hard to believe that after so many years of people creating and using special spaces for our ablutions, we are still finding new ways to pamper ourselves in such a necessary room. Technological advances as well as the incorporation of unexpected elements contribute to the never-ending reinvention of one of the most basic chambers in the home. Some of these advancements have a humorous edge to them: The toilet that senses a person's approach and raises its lid (or the toilet seat itself if so programmed) and then closes and flushes itself has been designed to end the "seat wars" between men and women. Other new models attempt to deal with the diminishing supply of fresh water by incorporating a dual-flush system; this allows the user to push one of two buttons that control the amount of water used for cleaning the bowl. Many of the trends on the following pages are just plain pretty, but they all make me wish I had another bathroom in my home so that I could add something new and wonderful. (For more information on featured products, see pages 296–301.)

ABOVE: A WARMING DRAWER DESIGNED FOR USE IN WET OR DRY AREAS, INDOORS OR OUT, CONTRIBUTES A PAMPERING ELEMENT TO THE BATH. THIS MODEL CAN BE SET TO A MAXIMUM TEMPERATURE OF 200°F AND HAS A TIMER THAT SHUTS OFF AUTOMATICALLY AFTER FOUR HOURS. IT HOLDS FOUR TOWELS OR ONE LARGE TERRY CLOTH ROBE.

OPPOSITE: THIS WARMING DRAWER IS DESIGNED SPECIFICALLY FOR INSTALLATION IN CABINETRY, SO IT COMES WITHOUT A DRAWER FRONT—YOU CHOOSE A DRAWER PANEL TO MATCH YOUR CABINETS. AVAILABLE IN TWO DEPTHS (21½ INCHES AND 39½ INCHES), IT HOLDS UP TO FOUR TOWELS. A TIMER SHUTS OFF THE HEAT AUTOMATICALLY AFTER TWO HOURS.

The perfect innovation FOR CATCHING UP ON THE NEWS WHILE GETTING READY FOR WORK,
THIS LCD HIGH-DEFINITION TV DISAPPEARS WHEN IT IS TURNED OFF SO YOU SEE ONLY A MIRROR SURFACE. THE
UNIT IS MOUNTED ON AN OFFSET BRACKET, WITH THE TELEVISION PARTIALLY RECESSED INTO THE WALL.

Watch your favorite program WHILE YOU BRUSH YOUR TEETH. THIS LCD TV/MIRROR COMBINATION SUITS A MORE TRADITIONAL SETTING, PRESENTED IN A FRAME SET FLUSH WITH THE WALL. THE MIRROR SHAPE AND FRAME STYLE CAN BE CUSTOMIZED. AN ALUMINUM INTERFACE PLATE THAT HOLDS THE MIRROR GLASS ABSORBS AND DISSIPATES THE HEAT FROM THE TELEVISION.

A mini kitchen OR BEVERAGE CENTER IN THE
MASTER SUITE OFFERS THE CONVENIENCE OF MORNING JUICE
OR AN ENERGY DRINK BEFORE YOU EMERGE TO GREET FAMILY
OR OVERNIGHT GUESTS. THE MINI FRIDGE IS ALSO HELPFUL FOR
KEEPING INSULIN OR OTHER MEDICATIONS CLOSE AT HAND.

Bars designed for KITCHENS OR FAMILY ROOMS HAVE FOUND THEIR WAY TO THE MASTER SUITE, WHERE THEY SERVE AS COFFEE STATIONS. ALL YOU NEED IS A CABINET, A SMALL SINK, COUNTERSPACE, AND AN ELECTRICAL OUTLET TO CREATE THIS PRACTICAL AMENITY.

Sinks are evolving INTO SCULPTURE EXECUTED WITH UNEXPECTED MATERIALS. THIS ONE IS COMPOSED OF SHAPED MARINE PLYWOOD WITH A CLEAR GLASS FRONT SEALED WITH SILICONE.

Make a statement WITH A POWDER ROOM SINK. THIS CUSTOM-DESIGNED COPPER TROUGH WITH A BLUESTONE RIM STRETCHES THE WIDTH OF THE ROOM. THE WATERFALL FAUCET REFLECTS A GROWING TREND TOWARD UNUSUAL WATER DELIVERY OPTIONS. A SINGLE LEVER ON THE BACKSPLASH (NOT VISIBLE HERE) CONTROLS THE FLOW AND TEMPERATURE OF THE WATER.

Old is new again. FABRICATED WITH A
FIRECLAY CONSOLE TOP AND SQUARE LEGS, THIS SINK
REFLECTS RENEWED INTEREST IN 1920S DESIGN. TO MEET
THE CURRENT DEMAND FOR CUSTOMIZATION, THE LEGS ARE
AVAILABLE IN A VARIETY OF COLORS.

Natural and organic shapes ARE INFLUENCING THE DESIGN OF VESSEL SINKS, WHICH CONTINUE TO EVOLVE. THIS MODEL RESEMBLES A CALLA LILY, AND ITS ASYMMETRICAL FORM HAS A DISTINCTLY CONTEMPORARY LOOK, ALMOST LIKE A PIECE OF MODERN SCULPTURE.

Exciting new fixture designs HAVE BEEN
BORROWED FROM COMMERCIAL APPLICATIONS AND BROUGHT INTO THE
MODERN HOME. IN A SHARED BATHROOM, THE SINK (BELOW) CAN BE
INTERLOCKED WITH ADDITIONAL ONES LIKE A JIGSAW PUZZLE TO SAVE
SPACE. IMAGINE MULTIPLE SIBLINGS, EACH WITH HIS OR HER OWN SINK.

Inspired by items AT THE SMITHSONIAN INSTITUTION, THESE HANDSOME
SINKS BRING CACHET TO THE POWDER ROOM OR BATHROOM. THE CARVED MARBLE BOWL
(BELOW) DRAWS ITS DESIGN FROM THE LIGHTING FIXTURES INSTALLED IN THE SMITHSONIAN
INSTITUTION BUILDING (THE CASTLE) IN 1915. THE SINK (OPPOSITE) FEATURES CUTWORK
DECORATION INSPIRED BY AN ENGLISH STRAWBERRY SERVER PRODUCED AROUND 1800. THE
DRAIN IS INVISIBLE UNDER THE PIERCED PATTERN AT THE BOTTOM OF THE BOWL.

An example of hip contemporary

EUROPEAN DESIGN, THIS PAIR OF SINKS REPRESENTS AN ARCHITECT'S
TAKE ON THE TRADITIONAL PEDESTAL SINK. THE BLOCKY GEOMETRIC
SHAPE WITH SOFTLY ROUNDED EDGES IS TIMELESS IN STYLE,
COMFORTABLE TO USE, AND EASY TO CLEAN.

Bidets are showing up IN NORTH AMERICAN BATHROOMS. THEY WERE INVENTED IN 18TH-CENTURY FRANCE AND ARE COMMON IN MANY EUROPEAN, LATIN AMERICAN, AND ASIAN COUNTRIES. FAVORED BECAUSE THEY FACILITATE PERSONAL HYGIENE AND HELP MINIMIZE TOILET PAPER USE, THEY'RE ALSO HANDY FOR SOAKING THE FEET. THIS STYLISH MODEL FEATURES A SINGLE-HANDLE WATER CONTROL. THE HOLE IN THE LID OF THE TOILET ALLOWS USERS TO RAISE THE LID WITHOUT TOUCHING THE RIM.

In the ongoing search FOR NEW FRONTIERS, DUAL-FLUSH TOILETS HAVE BEEN DEVELOPED. THIS TECHNOLOGY ENCOURAGES WISE WATER USE: USE LESS WHEN LESS IS NEEDED AND MORE FOR GREATER FLUSHING POWER. THE SPLIT BUTTON ON TOP OF THE TANK ALLOWS A CHOICE OF WATER VOLUME FOR EACH FLUSH.

This stylish toilet looks LIKE A HATBOX! INSTEAD OF A TANK, IT USES AN ELECTRIC PUMP TO PUSH WATER INTO THE BOWL TO FLUSH THE CONTENTS. ITS DIMENSIONS MAKE IT A GOOD CHOICE FOR A POWDER ROOM OR SMALL SECONDARY BATHROOM.

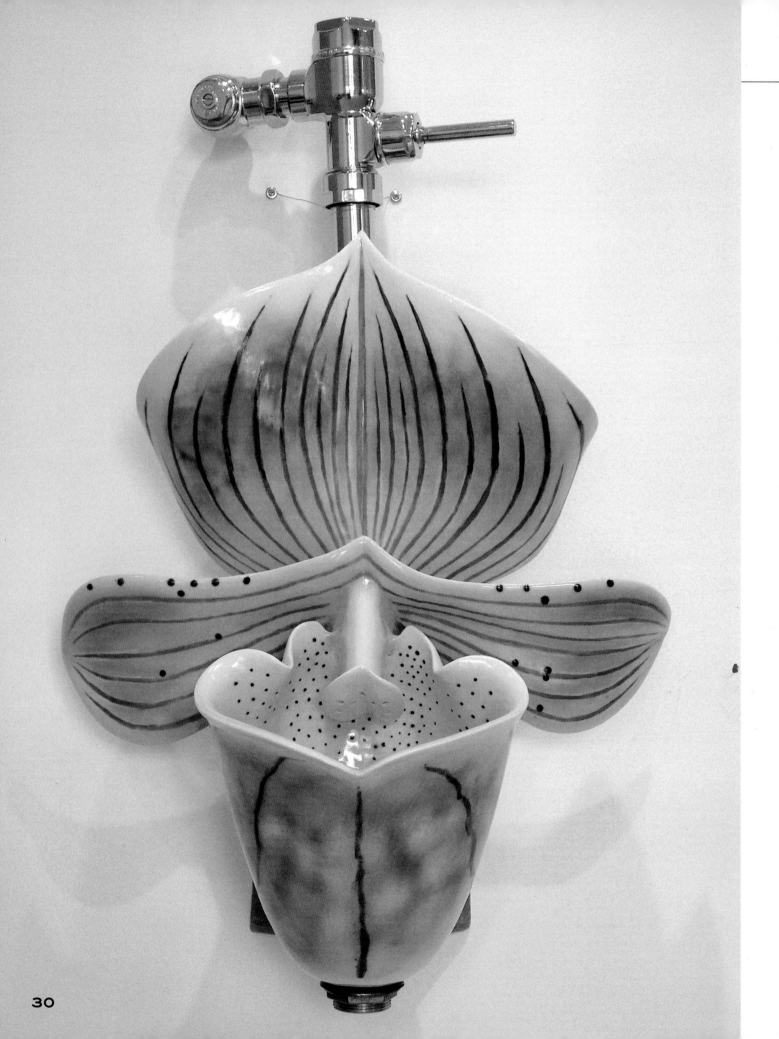

The new luxury item

IN THE BATH IS A URINAL, FINALLY ALLOWING
MEN TO HAVE A SAY IN A ROOM OFTEN
DOMINATED BY WOMEN'S NEEDS. ITEMS
OF ART AS WELL AS WHIMSY, THE NAUTILUS
SHELL (LEFT AND BELOW) AND ORCHID
(OPPOSITE) ARE HANDMADE AND TRULY
DISTINCTIVE PIECES OF SCULPTURE.

A more traditional

SHAPE FOR A URINAL HAS BEEN UPDATED
WITH LED LIGHTS EMBEDDED IN A MOLDED
POLYETHYLENE BOWL. THIS MODEL COMES
WITH AN AUTOMATIC FLUSHER HEAD AND IN A
VARIETY OF COLORS FROM PINK TO BLUE.

Now that urinals HAVE BROKEN OUT OF THE MEN'S ROOM, THERE SEEMS TO BE NO
END TO DESIGN POSSIBILITIES. THIS PIECE COMES IN MANY COLORS AND IS CAST FROM SOLID RESIN
FOR EXTRA STRENGTH. ALL THE PLUMBING IS HIDDEN INSIDE THE NARROW BASE.

Bathroom humor REACHES ITS ULTIMATE LEVEL WITH THIS URINAL, WHICH IS MADE OUT OF PRESSED GALVANIZED STEEL AND IS TITLED "PALE ALE." THE PLUMBING CAN COME UP THROUGH THE PLINTH OR STRAIGHT OUT OF THE WALL, AND THE PLINTH CAN BE MADE FROM A VARIETY OF MATERIALS, FROM LAMINATE TO STAINLESS STEEL AND SOLID WALNUT.

Light the way WITH LED LIGHTS THAT POP INTO THE TILE. THE WIRE IS LAID UNDER THE TILE AT INSTALLATION AND PLUGS INTO THE BACK OF THE LIGHT UNITS, WHICH ARE INSERTED FROM THE FRONT. WHEN THE LIGHT EVENTUALLY BURNS OUT, IT'S EASY TO PRY THE UNIT UP AND REPLACE THE LIGHT.

New technology BRINGS NEW APPLICATIONS. LUMINOUS GLASS BORDERS CAN BE USED WITH LED TILES OR ALONE TO HIGHLIGHT A STEP FOR SAFETY OR TO ADD AMBIENCE WITH INDIRECT LIGHT.

Chromatherapy COMBINES WITH THE LUXURY OF TOTAL BODY SUBMERSION IN THIS WHIRLPOOL TUB. WATER POURS INTO THE TUB FROM ON HIGH VIA A LAMINAR-FLOW BATH FILLER MOUNTED IN THE CEILING.

Imagine SINKING INTO A TUB FILLED TO THE BRIM—WITHOUT WORRYING ABOUT FLOODING THE HOUSE! THAT'S THE BEAUTY OF A TUB WITH AN OVERFLOW RESERVOIR.

Bathroom Elements

Sinks

Sinks have come a long way from the washbasin and pitcher. Here are some examples of the options available.

Left: A frosted-glass vessel sink brings the washbasin into the 21st century.

Opposite: Tucking the sink into a custom-built vanity that mimics a dresser gives this bath the look of a furnished living space. The paneled walls of the alcove camouflage cabinet doors. Dark wood imbues the space with a tailored look, while the gilt bow on the mirror and crystal drops on the sconces acknowledge a softer influence.

41

A VANITY WITH DRAWERS AND UNDERSINK STORAGE ELIMINATES THE NEED FOR MEDICINE CABINETS ABOVE THE SINKS. THIS FREES THE WALL FOR DRAMATIC, SPACE-ENHANCING MIRRORS. WITH UNDERMOUNTED SINKS, THE COUNTERTOP IS EASY TO KEEP CLEAN.

Sinks have evolved into a variety of forms, many of them extremely decorative. Housing the sink in a piece of furniture, whether it's custom-built cabinetry or a converted antique dresser, offers several advantages: drawers and cabinets for storing necessities, a box to hide the plumbing, and the opportunity to add architectural style to the room. The fluted pilasters and paneling on the vanity (opposite) take their cue from the classic style of the moldings that wrap the room and frame the windows.

Traditional bathroom cabinetry usually calls for either an undermounted sink (opposite) or a self-rimming sink that drops into a hole cut into the countertop. Vessel sinks are a third possibility: Sitting atop the cabinetry, they make a dramatic artistic statement while preserving the benefits of cabinet storage.

Another popular sink option is a pedestal or footed sink. This type can make a small chamber feel larger because it takes up less visual and physical space. Its fixtures and decorative details can help reinforce the overall decorating style and tone of the room.

A MIRROR ON A STAND
OR MOUNTED ON A
BRACKET ALLOWS YOU
TO PLACE A SINK IN
FRONT OF A WINDOW,
TAKING ADVANTAGE
OF LIGHT AND VIEWS.
NOTE THE SMALLER
MAGNIFYING MIRROR
THAT CAN SWING
FORWARD TO SUIT
YOUR VIEWING NEEDS.
(SEE PAGE 53 FOR
ANOTHER VERSION
OF THIS KIND OF
MIRROR.) A GENEROUS
COUNTERTOP
PROVIDES SPACE FOR
DISPLAYING PRETTY
TOILETRIES.

OPPOSITE: VESSEL SINKS HAVE BECOME INCREASINGLY POPULAR. THESE HAVE A FLAT BOTTOM THAT ADDS VISUAL WEIGHT AND A CLEAN LINE IN KEEPING WITH THE SLABLIKE CONSTRUCTION OF THE TUB. AN INDENTATION IN THE VANITY CREATES A HANDY ALCOVE FOR A TOWEL ROD.

LEFT: THIS MIRRORED VANITY REFLECTS THE INFLUENCE OF 1940S DESIGN, SPECIFICALLY HOLLYWOOD REGENCY STYLE. ALTHOUGH PROBABLY NOT WELL SUITED TO HOMES WITH SMALL CHILDREN (UNLESS YOU DON'T MIND FINGERPRINTS AND SMUDGES), A MIRRORED VANITY CAN ENHANCE THE ILLUSION OF LIGHT AND SPACE IN A SMALL BATHROOM. AND IT LOOKS UNCOMMONLY CHIC.

A FROSTED GLASS
BOWL ADDS
SUBTLE COLOR AND
SLEEK STYLE TO A
TRADITIONAL BATH.
WALLMOUNT FITTINGS
SAVE COUNTERSPACE
WITH A SINK LIKE THIS.
THE VANITY OFFERS
STORAGE BENEFITS
YET PRESERVES A
SPACIOUS FEELING
IN THE ROOM: THE
CABINETRY STOPS
SHORT OF THE FLOOR,
LEAVING ROOM BELOW
FOR BASKETS TO HOLD
TOWELS OR SUPPLIES.
THE WALLMOUNT
TOWEL WARMER IN THE
PASSAGE IS ANOTHER
MUST-HAVE FEATURE
FOR THE LUXURY BATH.

OPPOSITE: VESSEL SINKS HAVE ALLOWED A WHOLE NEW APPROACH TO THE TYPE OF FURNITURE USED IN A BATH. A SIMPLE WORKTABLE MORPHS INTO A SLEEK MODERN PIECE IN THIS CONTEMPORARY BATHROOM. THE BRUSHED METAL EXTERIOR OF THE BOWL RELATES TO THE SURFACE OF THE TABLE AND TO THE SOAP AND LOTION DISPENSERS, WHILE THE SHINY INTERIOR MATCHES THE FITTINGS AND TOWEL BAR.

LEFT: IN THIS VARIATION ON A FURNITURE-STYLE SINK, THE BUILT-OUT WALL CONTAINS THE LESS ATTRACTIVE ASPECTS OF THE PLUMBING AND PROVIDES A USEFUL SHELF. THE VANITY MOUNTS ON THE WALL, SO IT NEEDS ONLY TWO LEGS. THE WAVY APRON HIDES THE SINK TRAP AND ADDS A PLAYFUL ELEMENT TO THIS BASIC SPACE.

ABOVE: PEDESTAL SINKS TAKE UP LESS SPACE VISUALLY AND PHYSICALLY, SO THEY ARE GOOD CHOICES FOR SMALL ROOMS. A FRAMED FLOOR-TO-CEILING MIRROR FURTHER ENHANCES THE ILLUSION OF ROOMINESS.

OPPOSITE: SHAPED LEGS AND A SLIGHTLY SERPENTINE APRON TRANSLATE THE FEATURES OF A FARMHOUSE TABLE INTO PORCELAIN. THE COTTAGE STYLE OF THE SINK MARRIES WELL WITH A CONTEMPORARY FREESTANDING MIRROR.

Tubs & Showers

BEAUTIFULLY DESIGNED TUBS AND SHOWERS RAISE THE BASIC FUNCTION OF BATHING TO THE LEVEL OF SYBARITIC PLEASURE.

LEFT: TO MINIMIZE THE HEIGHT OF THIS TALL, NARROW SHOWER ALCOVE, THE FLOOR TILE EXTENDS PARTWAY UP THE WALL, SHORTENING THE VERTICAL AREA. A HORIZONTAL BAND ABOVE EYE LEVEL FURTHER SHRINKS THE ENCLOSURE TO HUMAN SCALE.

OPPOSITE: A FREESTANDING TUB IN FRONT OF A TALL WINDOW CREATES A THEATRICAL EFFECT, PLACING THE BATHER AT CENTER STAGE. ANTIQUE DOORS MOUNTED ON A SLIDING TRACK CAN COVER THE WINDOWS WHEN PRIVACY IS REQUIRED. MIRRORS IN THE FRENCH DOORS AND TRANSOMS PRESERVE PRIVACY TOO.

A MARBLE BOX ENCASES
THE PLUMBING AS WELL
AS THE UNDERMOUNTED
TUB. THE WIDE, FLAT
RIM SERVES AS BOTH
COUNTERSPACE AND
SEATING. A SEPARATE,
GLASS-ENCLOSED
SHOWER OCCUPIES THE
SPACE AT THE FOOT OF
THE TUB.

Bathrooms that possess a tub boast the most romantic part
of a washroom. The average bathroom lacks the space for a
freestanding tub, but if you have room to spare, a footed or
platform tub is the way to go for lots of drama. Freestanding
tubs offer a sculptural quality that helps define the style
of the room, from the curvaceous claw-foot tub of the
Victorian Era to the sleek ovals or rectangles designed by
contemporary architects. Boxed tubs require more space
to accommodate the framing and deck, but they offer the
convenience of a surface to hold necessities.

The easiest way to fit both a tub and shower into a
bathroom is to choose the 60×30-inch tub with shower that
has been a standard feature of suburban houses since the
1950s. In a larger bathroom, a separate tub and shower allow
you to tailor each fixture to a specific bathing experience—
luxurious soaking in a tub, thorough cleansing and water
massage in a shower. A separate shower also offers space
for built-in seating. A shower large enough to accommodate
two may need multiple water jets to create the steamy
warmth that is the chief appeal of a shower.

OPPOSITE: AN EXPANSIVE DECK AROUND THIS BUILT-IN TUB OFFERS DISPLAY SPACE FOR USEFUL AS WELL AS DECORATIVE ITEMS. DESIGNED TO FILL THE NICHE DOMINATED BY THE WINDOW, THE TUB IS POSITIONED FOR ENJOYING THE VIEW WITHOUT CONCERNS FOR PRIVACY.

ABOVE: TALK ABOUT GLAMOUR! THIS JEWEL OF A SOAKER IS A MOVIE STAR'S DREAM. THE REST OF THE ROOM HAS TO BE EQUALLY STUNNING BECAUSE THE MIRRORED PANELS ON THE TUB REFLECT THE ENTIRE BATH.

A TUB ON A PLATFORM
MAKES ROYAL TREATMENT
A REGULAR PART OF LIFE.
THIS ELABORATE BATH
SETUP IS ACTUALLY THE
GLAMOROUS RESULT OF A
BEDROOM CONVERSION.
THE FIREPLACE HAS BEEN
COVERED WITH MARBLE TO
CREATE A "HEADBOARD"
FOR THE TUB, WHICH
IS TOP-MOUNTED IN A
MARBLE-TOP BOX
THAT HIDES THE
PLUMBING LINES.

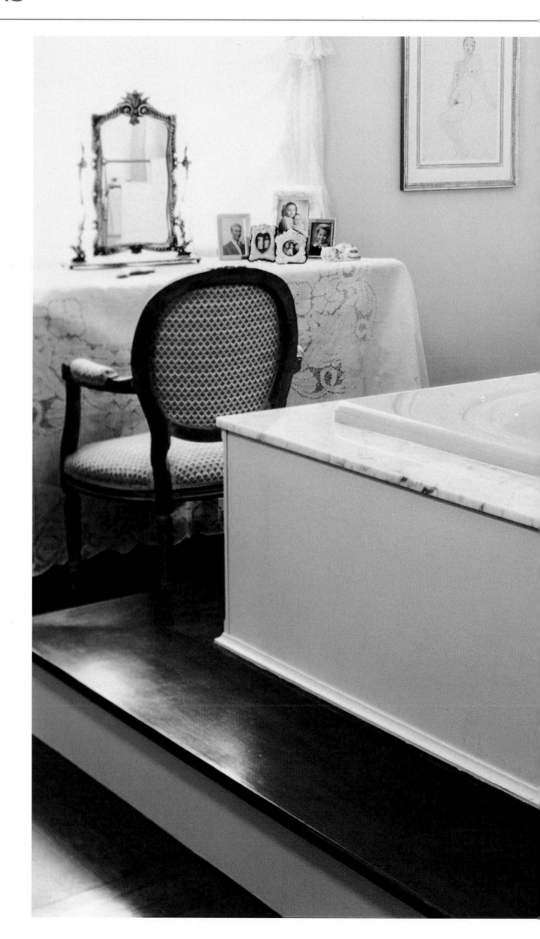

OPPOSITE: ADD ROMANCE AND SOFTNESS TO THE BATHROOM WITH AIRY NETTING SUSPENDED OVER A FREESTANDING TUB. THIS TYPE OF TENTLIKE CANOPY USUALLY HANGS OVER BEDS OR CRIBS YET IT WORKS JUST AS WELL IN THE BATHROOM.

ABOVE: TUBS ON FEET OR PLINTHS WERE COMMON IN THE BEGINNING OF THE LAST CENTURY. THEIR FREESTANDING SILHOUETTES STILL ADD CHARM TO A BATH. SHOWER CURTAIN SOLUTIONS ARE IMPERFECT, BUT THIS CIRCULAR ROD, CONNECTED TO THE CEILING AND THE SHOWERHEAD, OFFERS ONE OPTION.

An updated version of a footed tub, this egglike capsule brings visual simplicity to the modern bath. The sleek, tubular tub filler hides the plumbing pipes within the column, liberating the freestanding tub from a position close to the wall. The column also includes a handheld sprayer that facilitates hair washing or cleaning the tub. The sinks have minimal counterspace, but pullout shelves in the adjoining cabinets supply a surface for toiletries. A swivel-hinge freestanding towel bar allows towels to dry faster because air can circulate around them more easily.

ABOVE: WHAT COULD BE MORE ROMANTIC THAN SOAKING BY THE FIRE? WITH GAS LOGS, THE SIMPLE FLICK OF A SWITCH TAKES THE CHILL OFF THE ROOM AND LETS YOU ENJOY FLICKERING FIRELIGHT.

OPPOSITE: OVAL-SHAPED LIKE VINTAGE TUBS BUT STREAMLINED FOR A MORE MODERN LOOK, THIS TUB WORKS WELL IN A BATH WITH AN OLD-WORLD AMBIENCE. THE FAUCETS AND HANDHELD SHOWERHEAD (RESTING ON A TELEPHONE-STYLE CRADLE) ASSERT THE VINTAGE ROOTS OF THIS TUB DESIGN.

OPPOSITE: Evoking the black-and-white striped facades of Tuscan cathedrals, this gray-and-white tiled shower is a cathedral to cleanliness. Multiple water jets and showerheads can be programmed with the electronic control pad at the entrance.

ABOVE: A completely tiled room could feel closed in and cold; here, clear acrylic legs on the sinks and frameless glass walls on the shower ensure an open feeling. The large beveled mirror reflects light (and a view of the tub). "HIS" and "HERS" mosaic "rugs" in front of the sinks add a touch of humor.

RIGHT: AVAILABLE IN AN ARRAY OF SIZES, COLORS, AND FINISHES, TILES CAN TRANSFORM A PLAIN CUBICLE INTO AN INTERESTING ENCLOSURE. COVE MOLDING AT THE TOP AND BOTTOM OF THIS SHOWER STALL PROVIDES A TRANSITION BETWEEN THE HORIZONTAL AND VERTICAL SURFACES. A "PLATE RAIL" OF NARROW TILES DRAWS THE EYE FROM THE MAIN GRID OF SQUARES TO THE PLEASING HONEYCOMB PATTERN ABOVE.

OPPOSITE: BODY SPRAY PLATES SET INTO THE WALL AIM JETS OF WATER AT WHATEVER LEVEL YOU DESIRE.

Dressing Tables

PRETTY AS WELL AS FUNCTIONAL, DRESSING TABLES BRING AN ELEMENT OF LUXURY TO MASTER BATH SUITES AND BEDROOMS.

LEFT: DRESSING TABLES ARE THE LOGICAL SPOT TO DISPLAY PERFUMES AND TOILETRIES. THE PORCELAIN LABELS DECORATING THE CRYSTAL DECANTERS RECALL SILVER LABELS DESIGNED FOR LIQUOR DECANTERS.

OPPOSITE: CUT-CRYSTAL BOTTLES AND LAMPS AND BEVELED EDGES ON THE VANITY DRAWERS GLITTER LIKE DIAMONDS IN FRONT OF A MIRRORED WALL. SMOCKED LAMPSHADES AND A WHITE CHAIR COVER ADD SOFTNESS.

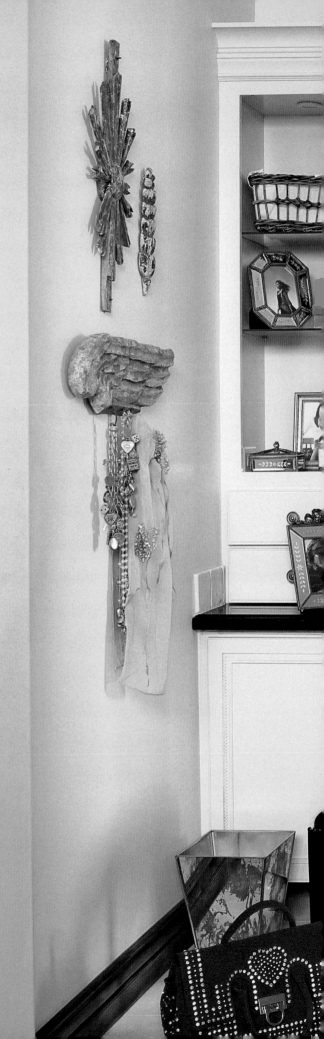

WHAT A WONDERFUL
JUXTAPOSITION OF
ROMANCE AND SAFARI!
THIS TRULY ECLECTIC
MARRIAGE—A HEART-
SHAPE VENETIAN GLASS
MIRROR PAIRED WITH A
BEVELED-EDGE MIRROR
FRAMED IN BLACK—
ENJOYS A PERFECT
UNION BECAUSE OF
THE UNDERSTATED
COMMONALITIES:
LIGHTING, CABINETRY,
AND SILVER
ACCESSORIES. THE
ZEBRA STRIPE ON THE
VANITY BENCH UNIFIES
THE COLOR SCHEME.

Dressing tables have many purposes beyond looking pretty. They offer a dedicated spot for putting on makeup, brushing hair, plucking, staring, and generally assessing what needs to be done after the bath. They supply a surface for arranging necessary and decorative toiletries and for resting a magnifying mirror (essential for some of those grooming tasks).

The advantage of placing a dressing table in the bathroom is the proximity to water, but they are convenient in bedrooms too, offering storage for jewelry and toiletries. If you're designing a bathroom from scratch, consider building a dressing table into the vanity cabinetry. Otherwise, an antique table or desk can serve the purpose. You need a countertop or tabletop that is 28 to 30 inches high with an open area underneath for your knees at least 24 inches high. You'll also need space in front of the dressing table for a chair or bench. Conventional wisdom calls for 36 inches, but I must confess that if I use a small bench, I can get by with 30 inches.

OPPOSITE: FOR A MORE CASUAL LOOK, BRUSH A COAT OF WHITE PAINT ON ALMOST ANY TABLE THAT'S 28 TO 30 INCHES HIGH, HANG A MIRROR ON THE WALL, AND—VOILÀ—YOU HAVE A DRESSING TABLE! ADD A SMALL TRAY WITH PERFUME BOTTLES, AND IT COMPLETES THE TRANSFORMATION.

ABOVE: IN THE ABSENCE OF A DRESSING TABLE, PRETTY PERFUME BOTTLES ARRANGED ON A SMALL TRAY WITH A GALLERY EDGE CAN BRING A SIMILAR EFFECT TO THE LAVATORY COUNTERTOP.

LEFT: In a nod to the 1940s, a capiz-shell coating brings shimmery elegance to a small dressing table. Angled in the corner, the distinctive table adds a feeling of luxury to a modest space.

ABOVE: Furniture covered in capiz shells can be hard to find, but lampshades, chandeliers, and decorative accessories that feature their pearlescent effects are readily available.

OPPOSITE: ONE WAY TO CREATE A DRESSING TABLE IS TO SKIRT AN EXISTING PIECE OF FURNITURE AND TOP IT WITH HEAVY GLASS. A MIRROR ON A STAND PROVIDES THE MEANS FOR PRIMPING.

ABOVE: MOVING BEYOND FROUFROU, THIS STREAMLINED VERSION OF A BUILT-IN VANITY IS EXECUTED WITH HIGH STYLE. THE DARK PANELING IS ILLUMINATED WITH TINY LOW-VOLTAGE PUCK LIGHTS THAT CAN BE RECESSED OR SURFACE-MOUNTED.

Powder Rooms 3

Powder Rooms

Although small, these rooms have become must-haves for any new home. Often called half baths, they offer full-size convenience.

Left: vessel sinks have become popular in part because they look more like attractive accessories than utilitarian objects.

Opposite: Architectural salvage lends itself to unique bathroom furniture, and the powder room is the place to indulge in dramatic effects. Here carved stone corbels support a blocky, trough-style sink in a room upholstered in a historic print.

Powder Rooms

RIGHT: TUCKING THE TOILET COMPARTMENT BEHIND A SLIDING DOOR ALLOWS MORE THAN ONE PERSON TO USE THE POWDER ROOM AT THE SAME TIME. A VENT FAN IN THE COMPARTMENT ENSURES SOUND-PROOFING FOR PRIVACY.

Beginning in the late 17th century, when a wig was essential to a properly dressed lady or gentleman, rooms were set aside for guests to repowder their wigs before entering the salon or ballroom. With the addition of plumbing, these spaces have morphed into the present-day powder room.

The luxury of a powder room allows guests to refresh themselves without trespassing on their host's territory. Powder room styles reflect the individual personality of the homeowner in a space small enough to allow for a more daring design than you might want in a larger bathroom.

Although they can have many extra luxuries, powder rooms require certain basic features. Aside from the obvious sink and toilet, the room needs a mirror for adjusting hair and makeup, fresh towels, fragrant soap, and a wastebasket. Hand lotion and facial tissues are thoughtful additions too.

BELOW: THE HEIGHT OF THIS BOWL REQUIRES A WALLMOUNT FAUCET, WHICH MAKES MORE ROOM ON THE COUNTERTOP FOR ACCESSORIES. THE MIRROR WAS CUSTOM DESIGNED TO FIT NEATLY BETWEEN THE SCONCES.

OPPOSITE: FILLING THE WALL BETWEEN THE WINDOWS WITH A MIRROR AND USING A TRANSPARENT SINK AND COUNTER MAGICALLY ENLARGE THIS SMALL SPACE.

ABOVE: AN ANTIQUE PIECE OF FURNITURE CREATES COUNTRY STYLE IN THIS LAVATORY. INSPIRED BY THE OLD BRONZE DRAWER PULL, THE SINK AND COUNTERTOP ARE COPPER, AND THE FAUCET IS OIL-RUBBED BRONZE.

ABOVE: MIRRORED WALLS, CEILING, AND LAVATORY EXPAND THIS SMALL ROOM WITH A DAZZLING PLAY OF REFLECTIONS.

OPPOSITE: THIS BATHROOM WITH PORTHOLE WINDOWS AND A VESSEL SINK SEEMS TO BE WELCOMING GUESTS WITH A BIG SMILE. PRACTICAL FEATURES INCLUDE A MIRROR THAT SWINGS OUT FROM THE WALL AND A SLEEK ONE-HOLE FAUCET WITH LEVER HANDLE.

Left: Clad in black marble with white fixtures, this powder room is confidently chic. The handles for the hot and cold water shutoff valves flanking the pedestal are just as dressy as the faucet handles and towel bar.

Opposite: To create architectural character in a small, plain room, thin glass tiles in a palette of grays and tans make up a dramatic backsplash that extends from floor to ceiling. The poured-concrete countertop and sink pick up the color of the medium-tone tiles, while the walls match the lightest ones.

OPPOSITE: DRAMA IN A POWDER ROOM NEED NOT MEAN GLAMOUR OR GLITZ. THIS VANITY, COMPOSED OF A PRIMITIVE-STYLE MEXICAN DRESSER WITH A FRENCH STONE-SLAB SINK, MAKES A STUNNING FOCAL POINT FOR THE ROOM. FROSTED-GLASS CORNUCOPIA SCONCES CONTRAST WITH THE RUSTIC MATERIALS AND SEVERE LINES.

BELOW: DARK-STAINED WOOD AND THE RUSTED PRESSED-METAL MIRROR FRAME CALL FOR A SIMILARLY RUSTIC FINISH ON THE BRIDGE FAUCET AND CROSS-POINT HANDLES. AN OILED-BRONZE FINISH WILL MELLOW WITH TIME, ALLOWING TARNISHED METAL TO PEEK THROUGH AS THE SURFACE AGES.

Traditional Appeal 4

Sumptuous Retreat

WITH A GENEROUS DOSE OF FRENCH FLAVOR, THIS BATH CONJURES UP ANOTHER TIME AND PLACE.

LEFT: A BUILT-IN DRESSING TABLE WITH PANELED DOORS AND DRAWERS OCCUPIES ONE END OF THE VANITY.

OPPOSITE: THE GARLAND MOTIF ON THE ANTIQUE DOORS INSPIRED THE CARVED FEATURES ON THE FRONT OF THE TUB SURROUND. AN ARTIST PAINTED THE CABINETS TO MATCH THE ORIGINAL AGED OCHER OF THE DOORS.

Sumptuous Retreat

RIGHT: TO SOFTEN THE SPACE, SHEER FABRIC FRAMES THE TUB, CREATING A HALF TESTER. THIS IS MORE THAN A DECORATIVE ADDITION; IT'S A CREATIVE PROBLEM SOLVER. BECAUSE A BATHROOM IS MOSTLY HARD SURFACES, IT CAN BE HARSH ACOUSTICALLY, AND THE FABRIC ACTS AS A SOUND BAFFLE.

Lack of imagination is the only thing (other than budget, space, and physics!) to restrict the scope of a bathroom design. This room reflects a particular decorating preference as well as an individual's practical needs. Generally, the style of the bath should reflect the rest of the residence, creating a seamless flow from the bedrooms to the baths. For a master bath I generally repeat the wall treatment and fabrics from the adjoining bedroom. This repetition creates the feeling of a master suite. It takes only one great detail to supply inspiration. Here the designer used a pair of carved 19th-century French château doors (see page 101) to set the general tone of the room. A French-style armchair adds to the overall Gallic flavor.

ABOVE: MIRRORS INSTALLED INSIDE THE RECESSED PANELS FUNCTION AS A LOOKING GLASS AT THE DRESSING TABLE AND REFLECT THE ROOM, ENLARGING THE SPACE AND INCREASING THE AMOUNT OF LIGHT CAST BY THE FIXTURES. FRAMING THE MIRRORS IN PANELING ACHIEVES AN ELEGANT EFFECT.

Elegant Outline

An Art Deco sensibility inspires a highly sophisticated space, creating the ambience of a glamorous boudoir.

Left: The bathtub deck is an ideal spot for interesting accessories. A large silver ewer is attractive as well as handy for rinsing your hair or the tub.

Opposite: A 1940s vase from Paris inspired the leaf-motif mosaic of the floor. This delicate tracery continues as a soft silver-green outline around the drawer panels.

When thinking about cabinet design, consider the overall appearance. How will the drawers and doors look when grouped together? Treat the whole ensemble as one big unit, not as individual components. Here the drawer framing on the sink vanity creates the look of one large recessed panel instead of lots of little ones, achieving a much more sophisticated style. This wonderful sense of scale extends to the dressing table (see page 105), where the bottom drawers are deeper and therefore visually heavier, anchoring the piece on reeded, shaped feet. Painting the small molding inside each panel outlines and emphasizes this design approach.

The same attention to detail is evident in the custom-designed tile floor. The leaf design, inspired by a 1940s vase, appears to be composed of two varieties of stone, but only one type of marble was actually used. Because marble, like any stone, is a natural material, its color can vary even within the same slab. Choosing only the lightest and darkest tiles of one kind of marble for the design creates the effect of a shadow, as if two different stones were used.

ABOVE: THIS CUT-GLASS VASE INSPIRED THE LEAF MOSAIC THAT DECORATES THE FLOOR OF THE BATHROOM.

OPPOSITE: A MIRRORED ALCOVE HOUSES GLASS SHELVING THAT DISPLAYS GLASS CONTAINERS. TO RELIEVE THE WALL OF CABINETRY, GLASS AND SOFTLY GATHERED FABRIC REPLACE THE PANELS ON THE UPPER DOORS. THE GLASS PROTECTS THE CABINET'S CONTENTS FROM DUST, AND THE FABRIC HIDES ANY CLUTTER.

Elegant Outline

Installing a shaped backsplash around a built-in tub adds a strong design detail without much effort. The silhouette can be almost anything that fits the size of the space. Pay attention to the edge detail of the backsplash; it can add a subtle flavor to the overall form. The Venetian mirror adds silvery glitter that echoes the sparkle of polished nickel and chrome fixtures.

Totally Tiled

WITH TILE ON EVERY SURFACE EXCEPT THE CEILING, THIS BATH HAS OLD-WORLD CHARM WITH A SLEEK TWIST.

LEFT: BEAUTIFUL MARBLE TILE MOSAICS CREATE THE BORDER SURROUNDING THE MAIN PART OF THE BATH FLOOR.

OPPOSITE: FRAMING IN AN ALCOVE FOR THE DRESSING TABLE CREATES A THREE-DIMENSIONAL SPACE FOR MIRRORS. BEVELED-MIRROR MEDICINE CABINETS MOUNTED OVER THE MIRRORED WALL HAVE HINGED DOORS THAT SWING OPEN TO LET YOU SEE THE BACK OF YOUR HEAD.

RIGHT: A SLAB OF MARBLE CAN BE CUT TO ALMOST ANY SHAPE. HERE IT FOLLOWS THE FORM OF THE SINK, ADDING OVERALL INTEREST TO THE DESIGN OF THE COUNTER. MATCHING THE FINISH ON THE LEGS AND THE FITTINGS UNIFIES THE LOOK OF THE LAVATORY AREA.

Welcome to the wonderful world of tile! As this bathroom demonstrates, tile now comes in many shapes, sizes, and textures—so many that you can cover every surface with it and produce an ensemble that's satisfyingly varied. Here tile creates architectural detail with bricklike wainscoting topped by a molded edge; it mimics wallpaper with alternating flat and reeded tiles; and it adds texture and pattern to the floor with a ruglike design edged by a mosaic border set within a grid of smaller tiles. The benefits of such a total immersion in tile? The material is durable and impervious to water and moisture. Wet tile can be slick, however, so for use on a bathroom floor, choose smaller sizes; the grout lines will help make the surface more slip-proof. This is especially important in the shower.

Glass, marble, and brushed metal might seem severe partners for so much tile. However, texture—the reeded and beveled-edge tiles and acid-washed marble—keeps the room from seeming cold. Cottage-style fixtures and lighting convey extra warmth and comfort.

OPPOSITE: THE MARBLE COUNTERTOP HAS BEEN ACID WASHED TO REMOVE THE SOFTER COMPONENTS OF THE STONE. THIS CREATES A TEXTURED SURFACE LESS LIKELY TO SCRATCH OR SHOW MARKS. THE CABINET DRAWERS AND SIDES ARE MADE OF REEDED GLASS THAT HAS BEEN SANDBLASTED ON THE INSIDE, CREATING A BLUE-GREEN COLOR THAT REFLECTS THE TONES OF THE FLOOR.

OPPOSITE: THIS SHOWER BOASTS A NICHE FOR SHAMPOO, A FRAMED AND TILED SPACE POSITIONED BETWEEN TWO WALL STUDS. BEVELED-EDGE BRICK-SHAPE TILES CAPPED WITH TILE MOLDING CREATE THE EFFECT OF WAINSCOTING, CONTINUING THE LINE OF THE HALF-WALL AROUND THE STALL.

ABOVE: THE DART-AND-BALL FEET ON THE SINK CONSOLE REINFORCE THE 1920S INFLUENCE EVIDENT IN THE OVERALL ROOM DESIGN. WHEN PLUMBING DETAILS SUCH AS SHUTOFF VALVES AND TRAPS ARE EXPOSED, THEY SHOULD MATCH THE FIXTURES, LIKE THESE IN BRUSHED NICKEL, SO THE DESIGN LOOKS INTENTIONAL RATHER THAN PURELY FUNCTIONAL.

Crystal & Glass

ROBIN'S EGG BLUE WALLS, CRISP WHITE TRIM, AND AN ABUNDANCE OF MIRROR AND GLASS MAKE THIS SUITE AN AIRY, LIGHT-FILLED RETREAT.

LEFT: A VENETIAN MIRROR ADDS GLIMMER TO THE SPACE.

OPPOSITE: THE VIEW TOWARD ONE END OF THE ROOM IS FRAMED BY A LARGE OPENING INTO THE TUB AREA. A GILDED IRON ÉTAGÈRE FOR TOWEL STORAGE MIMICS THE CURVY LINES OF THE CHANDELIER.

CRYSTAL & GLASS

RIGHT: A LARGE MIRROR AT THE END OF THE HALL REFLECTS THE WHOLE BATH, CREATING THE ILLUSION OF OPENING INTO ANOTHER ROOM. PAINTING THE MIRROR FRAME TO MATCH THE WOODWORK CAMOUFLAGES THE FRAME AS AN ARCHITECTURAL DETAIL.

Architectural niches assign tasks to individual areas, creating attractive vignettes throughout this bath. Separate spaces house the shower, toilet, and dressing table, and the sinks and tub occupy a space large enough for a seating area. With the toilet and shower set apart, the tub/sink area feels more like a boudoir/sitting room, an elegant twist on the typical loo.

The crisp white of the upholstered armchairs and cabinetry acts as a fresh foil against the robin's egg blue of the walls. This blue is particularly pretty reflected in mirrors because the color is reminiscent of thick glass.

Using rugs in a bathroom softens the space visually, physically, and acoustically. A small Oriental rug in front of the tub brings a warmer neutral to the palette.

Above: Walls and a built-in bench turn the shower niche into a small, separate room. The door casing is marble shaped to resemble wood molding and extends from the crown molding to the baseboard to duplicate the vertical emphasis of the corner pilasters.

ABOVE: THE ULTIMATE LUXURY IN A BATHROOM IS FURNITURE SUCH AS A CHEST OF DRAWERS OR CHAIRS. SEATING MAKES THE ROOM FEEL LIKE A LIVING SPACE AND ALLOWS A SPOUSE OR FRIEND TO PERCH IN COMFORT WHILE YOU GET READY FOR A PARTY.

OPPOSITE: A THEME OF LIGHT REFRACTION REPEATS THROUGHOUT THE SPACE, CULMINATING WITH THIS PRETTY DRESSING TABLE TRIMMED WITH MIRROR PANELS. EVEN THE LEGS HAVE MIRRORS SET INTO RECESSED PANELS TO REFLECT LIGHT.

Pretty as a Picture

Artwork in the bathroom and dressing room delights the eye and embellishes these spaces with an extra touch of elegance.

Left: The top of the dressing table is a reverse-painted mirror. An artist painted the back of the glass with a border pattern; then the back was silvered by a glass company to create the reflective surface.

Opposite: Hanging an oil painting over the tub creates a theatrical focal point. The paneled walls flanking the mirror in the tub enclosure conceal storage.

RIGHT: A CORNER SINK SET AGAINST AN ANGLED CORNER WALL OFFERS THE OPPORTUNITY TO INSTALL STATIONARY MIRRORS ON THE SIDE WALLS AND A HINGED-MIRROR MEDICINE CABINET IN THE CENTER. THIS ARRANGEMENT ALLOWS EASY REAR VIEWING.

The bathroom is more humid than other rooms in the house, so how can you showcase collections of art or special pieces there? Moisture-resistant artwork, such as art tiles, vintage ceramicware, or garden ornaments, is the answer. These objects can bring personality, pattern, and style to any bath. Hanging oil paintings is more unexpected and adds undeniable richness to the space.

In this bathroom the shower and toilet occupy separate spaces, allowing the tub and vanity area to feel more like a boudoir/lounging chamber than a water closet. Upholstered seating adds comfort or simply a convenient place to toss a robe or towel.

If a double vanity is too big for a space, tucking two separate ones into the corners of the room may be a viable alternative. When this room was renovated, the corners were framed diagonally to accommodate the pair of bowfront cabinets. Placing a sink in the corner provides a three-surface wall area for a hinged mirror. This is wonderfully practical for seeing the back of your head and creates an attractive framework for each vanity.

ABOVE: A SEPARATE DRESSING AREA OFF
THE BATHROOM INCLUDES A DRESSING
TABLE BUILT INTO A NICHE BETWEEN THE
CLOSETS. THE THREE SIDES OF THE NICHE ARE
MIRRORED, AND FOR ADDED VISUAL INTEREST
A DECORATIVE GILDED MIRROR HANGS OVER
THE BACK SECTION. LAYERING MIRRORS OVER
MIRRORS IS A CLASSIC DECORATOR'S TRICK
FOR CREATING A FEELING OF RICHNESS.

Study in Black & White

As this marble and tile bathroom illustrates, sometimes no color is all the color you need.

Left: A mosaic border adds an element of traditional elegance to a room that blends classic and modern styles.

Opposite: Oiled, brushed-bronze stands hold solid stone sinks. For an unexpected touch of levity, octopuses drape the faucets. Sconces dripping with pure black crystals add glamour. Beveled mirrors enhance the effect.

STUDY IN BLACK & WHITE

A CLASSIC COMBINATION, BLACK AND WHITE, CREATES A COHESIVE DESIGN IN THIS BATHROOM. PHOTOS OF PICASSO, FRAMED IN BLACK AND MATTED IN WHITE, ARE GRAPHIC ENOUGH TO MAKE AN IMPACT AGAINST BOLDLY PATTERNED MARBLE. THE BLACK BENCH AND DRESSING TABLE AND BLACK MARBLE MOLDINGS GIVE THE EYE PLACES TO REST.

Various materials can bring pattern into a room: tile borders, wallpaper, fabric, clothes in a heap on the floor. Alternatively, consider using the patterns inherent in natural stone. For example, oversize rectangular marble tiles, installed to avoid matching up any veining, yield a boldly patterned surface. The overall effect is surprisingly soft in color, belying the smooth hardness of the marble.

Using jet-black glass for the prisms, arms, and bobeches of the light fixtures (see page 127) jazzes up the tone of the room and plays down the hard edges of the sink consoles by adding a traditional element. Round mirrors create a pleasing foil to the rectilinear sinks while retaining the purity of simple form used throughout the bath. This concept of simple shapes repeats in the straight-edged block of the tub and the elliptical form of the toilet, creating a look that is as modern as the artist whose image graces the walls.

Vintage View

Mixing quartersawn wood and rich brown marble creates a tailored yet earthy environment for soaking.

LEFT: This Shaker-inspired vanity is built from quartersawn oak. The straight graining results from the way the wood is milled.

OPPOSITE: An upstairs shower with a private view enjoys the novel benefit of a functioning window. Marble on the windowsill provides another spot for shampoos and soaps. The surface of the marble floor is honed to minimize slipperiness when it's wet.

VINTAGE VIEW

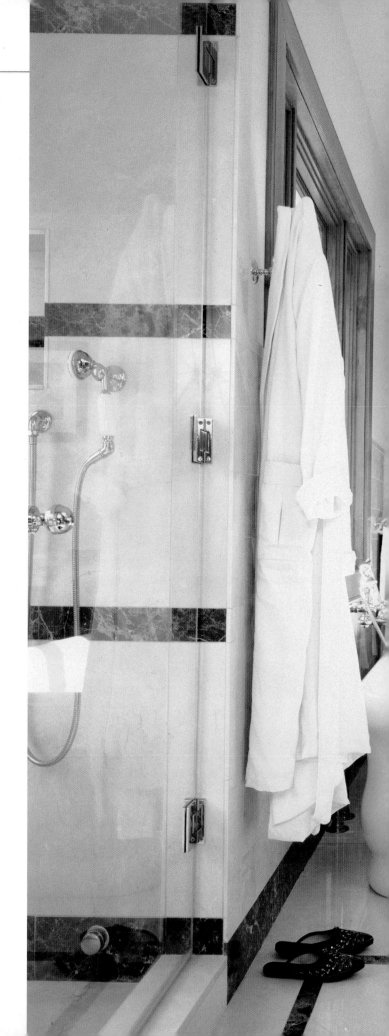

SINKS SET INTO
FURNITURE-STYLE
VANITIES ARE SEPARATED
BY FRENCH DOORS. THE
FLOOR'S BROWN MARBLE
BORDER SKIRTS THE TUB
AND VANITIES, CLEARLY
MARKING DIFFERENT USE
ZONES.

Bathrooms with a vintage feel offer an antidote to the stresses of contemporary life. The spirit of a previous era reveals itself in various details, from the way tile is laid to the style of the cabinetry. One detail that gives bathroom furniture a more vintage look is old-fashioned-looking hardware. On these vanities, glass knobs on the doors and drawers are reminiscent of 1930s-style fittings. Mounting the faucets on the walls is another quaint component that adds to the old-time flavor of this space. (Wallmount faucets have come back into vogue with the popularity of vessel sinks, so they have a modern aspect as well.) The curvaceous shape of the tub, reminiscent of Victorian fixtures, and the straightforward Shaker-style lines of the vanities bring together contrasting design sensibilities to create a room that respects the past.

The deep brown tones of marble paired with creamy beige tile accent the warmth of the wood vanities and trimwork. Dividing the shower wall with horizontal strips of brown marble creates a strong visual element that repeats on the floor, uniting the design of the room.

Arched
Triumph

OLD-WORLD INFLUENCES AND A NEUTRAL PALETTE
IMBUE A MASTER BATH WITH QUIET ELEGANCE.

LEFT: FOUND IN AN
ANTIQUES STORE,
THE PAINTED DOORS
LEADING INTO THE
MASTER SUITE ARE
FROM 19TH-CENTURY
ITALY.

OPPOSITE: A COVED
CEILING BLURS THE
ROOM'S HEIGHT,
CREATING WARMTH
WHILE PRESERVING
A FEELING OF
OPENNESS.
THE BUILT-IN
DRESSING TABLE
IS CONVENIENTLY
CLOSE TO THE SINK.
USING A SMALL
FREESTANDING
MIRROR AT THE
TABLE LEAVES THE
WALL ABOVE FREE
FOR ARTWORK
THAT SOFTENS THE
UTILITARIAN ASPECTS
OF THE SPACE.

ABOVE: THE CUSTOM-BUILT TOWEL CABINET IN THE WING BESIDE ONE VANITY MIMICS A FREESTANDING HUTCH. TEXTURED GLASS ENHANCES THE ANTIQUE LOOK.

OPPOSITE: THE CUSTOM-DESIGNED BOWFRONT VANITY ACCENTS THE SHAPE OF THE SINK. THE CUTOUT FEET MAKE THE CABINETS LOOK LIKE FURNITURE.

OPPOSITE: AN ARCHED NICHE RELIEVES THE ANGLED WALL JOINING THE TWO VANITY AREAS. THE SHOWER ENCLOSURE IS BEHIND THE NICHE.

ABOVE: THE ARCH THEME REPEATS THROUGHOUT THE SPACE, REFLECTING AN OLD-WORLD, MEDITERRANEAN INSPIRATION. A NEW MIRROR WITH AN ANTIQUE LOOK HANGS ABOVE AN ANTIQUE FRENCH BENCH WITH A NEEDLEPOINT CUSHION.

Glamour 5

Star Treatment

FROM CONCAVE VANITY FRONTS TO ROUND MIRRORS HUNG HIGH, CAREFULLY PLACED SILHOUETTES CREATE A STRIKING IMPACT IN THIS BATHROOM.

LEFT: THIS CHANDELIER LOOKS LIKE A COLLECTION OF CRYSTAL MARTINI STIRRERS BOUND TOGETHER FOR A DAZZLING EFFECT.

OPPOSITE: UPHOLSTERING THE WALL BEHIND THE BANQUETTE WITH MATCHING FABRIC ADDS PIZZAZZ (AND ON A MORE MUNDANE LEVEL, ABSORBS SOUND).

Star Treatment

BUILT-IN FRAMED
MIRRORS EMBRACE THE
VANITIES, CREATING
THE ILLUSION OF AN
ADJACENT ROOM.
INSTALLING MIRRORS
IN THIS FASHION
TREATS THEM AS
AN ARCHITECTURAL
ELEMENT RATHER THAN
AN ACCESSORY. THE
ROUND MIRROR ABOVE
SUGGESTS A PORTHOLE
WINDOW INTO THE
ILLUSORY ADJOINING
ROOM.

Cary Grant would have looked right at home in this bathroom. Its over-the-top elegance seems to scream Hollywood.

Mirrors behind each vanity and below the crown molding create illusions of extended space. The overscale round mirrors update a motif popular in 19th-century houses, when circle details embellished doors and windows. In the bay around the tub, custom-painted glass panels provide privacy and reflect the tub from every angle.

Dresser-style vanities in rich, dark wood give the room a furnished look. White marble vanity tops create a visual connection with the tumbled-marble floor and white porcelain tub. Nickel sconces, faucets, and vanity knobs accent the space with a silvery gleam that's cool and understated.

Floor-length draperies emphasize the height of the ceiling, making a dramatic backdrop for the tub. Using fabric wherever possible in a large bath helps soften the acoustics created by the many hard surfaces. The built-in banquette and upholstered wall (see page 145) help baffle sound as well. If possible, use slipcovers on furniture in a bath; when they are soiled, the covers can be thrown in the wash along with the towels.

RIGHT: THE DRESSING ROOM AND SHOWER DOORS RECEIVE EQUAL ARCHITECTURAL TREATMENT, SO THEY CLAIM EQUAL VISUAL IMPORTANCE. THE SAME MOLDING ALSO FRAMES THE WALL MIRRORS FOR CONTINUITY.

BELOW: RECTANGULAR TILES BORDER THE DIAMOND-SET MARBLE SQUARES OF THE MAIN FLOOR, CREATING THE SUGGESTION OF A RUG.

Classic
Opulence

An astute assemblage of motifs from the past results in a luxurious room for bathing and dressing.

LEFT: Carved-stone trim caps the tumbled-marble tile that continues from the floor up the wall to create a wainscoting.

OPPOSITE: This French cast-iron tub is mounted on a concrete base, high enough to take in the view. The base was formed with a traditional profile to blend with the classic moldings that frame the window.

Classic Opulence

MIRRORED LATTICEWORK FLANKS THE CENTER MIRROR AT THE DRESSING TABLE. THE LATTICE DESIGN WAS CLEVERLY COPIED FROM THE ARMOIRES AND MODIFIED TO INCLUDE AN OVAL FRAME FOR A WALLMOUNT SCONCE IN EACH PANEL.

Classical columns, garden urns, a custom wall finish, and tumbled marble create an aged effect of beauty and grace in this 22-foot-long master bath and dressing room suite. A café au lait color palette establishes a soothing atmosphere and relies on subtle textural differences of stone and inlaid wood to add variety.

Custom-built closets form the core of the room and custom armoires stand along three walls, providing an abundance of storage that organizes clothing by category: undergarments, suits, shirts, ties, and accessories. The cupboard doors are covered with mirrors, bouncing light around the room and enlarging the sense of space. The built-in units have simple recessed panels holding the mirrors, while the freestanding armoires have latticework doors recalling 18th-century English china cabinets. Both built-ins and armoires are treated with the same rubbed, decorative paint finish for a uniform appearance.

Floor-to-ceiling columns introduce a sense of architectural grandeur and define the room's classical roots. Rather than being set on square plinth blocks, the bases are round to avoid the possibility of stubbed toes.

Classic Opulence

RIGHT: A NEW GARDEN URN, FITTED WITH STANDARD PLUMBING FIXTURES, SERVES AS A SINK. AN ANTIQUE URN STANDS A FEW FEET AWAY. THE FLOOR OF ITALIAN MARBLE TILES IS LAID IN A CLASSIC ROMAN PATTERN OF OCTAGONS AND SQUARES THAT CONTINUES UP THE WALL TO FORM A LOW WAINSCOTING.

LEFT: THE DECORATIVE PAINT TREATMENT ON THE WALLS SUGGESTS AGED, STAINED PANELING. A WALLMOUNT BRIDGE FAUCET WITH CROSS-POINT HANDLES AND PORCELAIN BUTTONS ACCOMMODATES THE DISTANCE BETWEEN THE SINK AND THE WALL.

ABOVE: THE TUB, DISCOVERED IN A FRENCH CHÂTEAU, RESTS ON A PEDESTAL TO TAKE ADVANTAGE OF THE VIEW. A FOOTSTOOL IN FRONT SUPPLIES THE NECESSARY BOOST TO CLIMB IN AS WELL AS A PLACE FOR TOWELS.

Breaking the Rules

WARM AND COOL NEUTRALS SELDOM MIX, BUT IN THIS BATHROOM THE PARTNERSHIP PRODUCES STUNNING RESULTS.

LEFT: A MOSAIC "RUG" DOMINATES THE SHOWER WALL AND SERVES AS THE ROOM'S FOCAL POINT. THE CONTRAST IN SCALE BETWEEN THE SMALL TILES OF THE MOSAIC AND THE LARGER WHITE MARBLE TILES AROUND IT IS KEY TO THE MOSAIC'S IMPACT.

OPPOSITE: THE LIMESTONE FLOOR INSPIRED THE CREAM COLOR OF THESE CABINETS. CROWN MOLDINGS THAT STOP SHORT OF THE CEILING CREATE THE EFFECT OF UNFITTED FURNITURE.

157

Breaking the Rules

The silk valance hangs on robe hooks instead of a curtain rod for a twist on a traditional window treatment. Mosaic tile trim repeats the tilework in the shower (see page 160).

Neutral palettes usually fall into the cool range (silvery grays, taupe, or lavender-tinted whites) or the warm range (cream, ivory, gold). In this bathroom, cool, gray-veined white marble paves the walls, while warm, creamy limestone covers the floor, producing a sophisticated mix that is traditional and elegant yet unexpected. For rich, decorative detail, mosaics of limestone tiles in black, cream, and gold border the tub and embellish the shower wall and seat. The shower seat is designed to help make the small shower stall feel larger. Covering the base with diamond-shape tiles points the eye upward, creating the illusion of greater height.

For added architectural interest, an arched header frames in the tub area at the bay window. Resting on the shelving units that flank the bath, it encloses the soaking space to create an intimate atmosphere for lolling.

An upholstered ottoman covered in faux suede offers a soft counterpoint to all the hard surfaces. It can be washed with soap and water, making it a practical yet luxurious choice.

159

ABOVE: RECTANGULAR WHITE MARBLE TILES FORM A SMOOTH BACKDROP FOR A WALL MOSAIC OF LIMESTONE TILES FRAMED WITH BLACK STONE.

OPPOSITE: BOOKCASE-STYLE SHELVES AND A PANELED SURROUND GIVE THE TUB THE LOOK OF FURNITURE.

Circular Motion

Constructed in what was originally a nautilus-shape room, this elegant master bath evolves into a sumptuous spalike retreat.

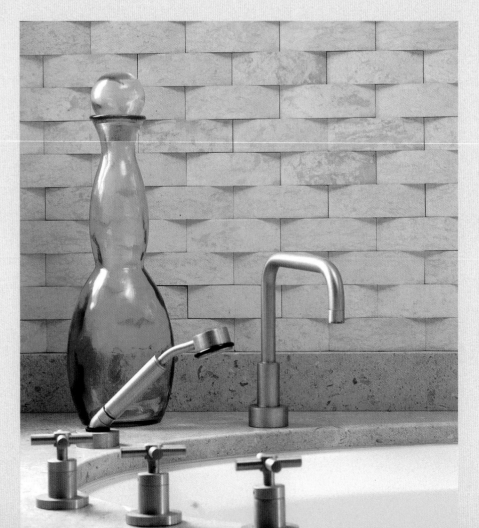

Left: Limestone tile laid in a staggered pattern creates the effect of woven stone. The rough texture plays off the grass cloth of the walls (opposite).

Opposite: Each of the two vanities in the room is flanked by a custom-designed walk-in closet. This closet is adjacent to a compartment for the toilet and bidet.

Circular Motion

One of two matching curved vanities separates one walk-in closet from the shower enclosure. Clad in subway tiles, the shower features a rain-shower head.

Originally a room that curled like a nautilus shell, this bathroom has been reworked into a circle and now accommodates all the required bath and spa elements in a radial floor plan. Built-in shelving units define the passage from the master bedroom and provide storage for accessories and towels. Custom-designed matching curved vanities stand directly opposite each other, balancing the room and allowing the owners separate personal areas. Open cubbies under each sink keep towels handy.

For a sophisticated, spalike atmosphere, the palette is restricted to dark neutrals, with the textures of grass cloth, tile, and limestone providing visual punch. To introduce the subtle shimmer that enlivens the matte finishes, a capiz-shell chandelier hangs in the center of the space; mother-of-pearl accessories add a luminous finish at countertop level, and silver drawer pulls and mirror frames contribute sparkle.

Lighting supplies high dramatic impact over the whirlpool tub, where convex tiles laid in a staggered pattern create a basket-weave effect. Recessed accent lights in the ceiling emphasize the highlights and shadows of the weave, giving the wall a graphic, sculptural look.

OPPOSITE: A BUILT-IN STORAGE UNIT DEFINES THE PASSAGE FROM THE MASTER BEDROOM INTO THE MASTER BATH. CUSTOM-DESIGNED TO MATCH THE VANITIES, THE UNIT OFFERS STORAGE AND DISPLAY SPACE.

ABOVE: SET INTO A LIMESTONE SURROUND, THE WHIRLPOOL TUB ENJOYS THE SPOTLIGHT UNDER A DRAMATIC WALL TREATMENT. A SOPHISTICATED TAKE ON THE TILE MURAL CONCEPT, THE WALL FEATURES CONVEX TILES LAID IN A BASKET-WEAVE PATTERN; RECESSED CEILING FIXTURES BRING OUT THE SCULPTURAL EFFECT. A CUSTOM-DESIGNED OTTOMAN WITH NAILHEAD EMBELLISHMENT ADDS TO THE RICH COMFORT OF THE SPACE.

ABOVE: STRINGS OF CAPIZ-SHELL DISKS CLUSTER THICKLY AROUND CONCEALED LIGHTING IN THE CHANDELIER, WHICH HANGS FROM A RECESS IN THE CEILING.

OPPOSITE: CUSTOM-BUILT FROM ASH AND STAINED A WARM, MIDTONE BROWN, EACH VANITY OFFERS AMPLE STORAGE SPACE SO THE LIMESTONE COUNTERS CAN REMAIN CLEAR OF TOILETRIES.

ABOVE: SQUARE, BRUSHED-NICKEL DRAWER PULLS WITH CIRCULAR CUTOUTS PROVIDE SUBTLE EMBELLISHMENT FOR THE ASH CABINETRY.

OPPOSITE: THE SUBTLE SHEEN OF BRUSHED-NICKEL FIXTURES AND THE SILVER-LEAF MIRROR FRAME BALANCE THE ROUGH TEXTURES OF GRASS-CLOTH WALLCOVERING AND A LIMESTONE COUNTERTOP.

French Polish

An antique French Empire dresser inspires the elegant furnishings and finishes in a stately master suite.

Left: A heated towel bar holds bath towels right outside the walkthrough shower, which connects both sides of the master bath.

Opposite: An antique Empire dresser in crotch mahogany veneer inspires the design for the tub surround. A mirrored closet door repeats the graceful lines of the Palladian window and tricks the eye into thinking there is another room beyond.

FRENCH POLISH

IN CONTRAST TO THE PERIOD STYLE OF THE VANITIES AND THE FAUCETS, THE MIRRORS ARE SIMPLE CHROME-FRAMED SQUARES. MOUNTED ON CHROME BARS, THE MIRRORS CAN BE TILTED TO ADJUST THE VIEW.

Cabinetry inspired by an antique French Empire dresser gives this master bath an old-world elegance. Taking a cue from the heirloom piece that sits under a Palladian window, furniture makers built a matching double-sink vanity and tub surround, using book-matched crotch mahogany veneer and a rich French polish finish. Achieved by hand-rubbing many layers of shellac onto the wood over a period of days, the finish seals the wood sufficiently to withstand the moisture of a bathroom. Because shellac is a natural product, it brings out the grain and beauty of the wood in a way that chemical lacquers do not. Matching the nickel finish of the tassel pulls to the faucets emphasizes the furniture quality of the vanities. The honed black granite of the countertops resembles the black marble top on the antique piece.

On the floor, honed crema marfil marble was used instead of limestone because it's more resistant to stains. Small black granite tiles serve as accents and connect the floor visually to the counters.

The floor treatment also continues through a short passage to the shared shower, unifying the spaces. Shared showers are a practical and increasingly popular way to connect individual suites while allowing each person the luxury of space and storage tailored to his or her needs.

Wood Traditions

Dark wood paneling dresses up a large bathroom, bringing it down to human scale and adding visual warmth and depth.

Left: A window bench forms a bridge between two cabinets, which serve as vanities in this spacious bath. The room is large enough to accommodate a small tea table in front of the window seat.

Opposite: Furnished with a thick Tibetan rug, framed prints, and an antique-inspired desk and chair, this room seems almost incidentally a bathroom.

WOOD TRADITIONS

Rich wood paneling adds elegance and luxury to a bathroom. When deciding how dark the stain should be, consider how much light the room receives and what materials can be used for color contrast. This space has a large window that washes the chamber in light, so dark walnut paneling creates an air of refined elegance rather than cavelike enclosure. Carrara marble counters and a travertine floor provide strong contrast that creates a visual foil for the space.

To keep the 17-foot-high ceiling from feeling overpowering in this relatively small room, the paneling extends only to 9 feet. This stops the eye at the top of the dark wood, bringing the bath down to a more human scale. Ironically, high ceilings in small spaces can make them feel smaller, so using molding, paneling, or a change of paint colors at a height of 9 or 10 feet is a particularly useful technique in narrow rooms, to avoid the feel of an elevator shaft.

Rather than placing the tub in front of the soaring window, that spot is devoted to a bench that conceals extra storage under its hinged lid (see page 176). The tub occupies the center of the room, sharing a wall with the shower. Installing a glass wall between the bath and shower makes the shower chamber feel more open and permits a view to the television mounted on the opposite wall (not shown).

Swimming in Luxury

INSPIRED BY ASIAN THEMES, THIS BATHING SUITE INDULGES IN A FLAIR FOR THE EXOTIC.

LEFT: AN ASIAN-STYLE BENCH HOLDS TOWELS AND OTHER ESSENTIALS AT THE END OF A SUNKEN BATHTUB.

OPPOSITE: TAKING A BATH IS MORE LIKE TAKING A DIP IN THIS SUNKEN SPA TUB. THE TUB DESIGN AND CENTRAL POSITION DICTATED THE REST OF THE ROOM DESIGN.

SWIMMING IN LUXURY

THE OVERSIZE SUNKEN TUB IS SET INTO A FLOOR OF CROSSCUT TRAVERTINE AND KALAHARI RED MARBLE, BANDED BY FINE STRIPS OF STAINLESS STEEL. WIDE FRENCH DOORS CRAFTED FROM MAHOGANY LEAD TO A PATIO COMPLETE WITH OUTDOOR KITCHEN.

Originally a kitchen and breakfast nook with no west-facing windows to catch the breezes or views, this lavish master bath now embraces the outdoors through expansive windows and oversize doors. Inside, a sunken tub establishes an exotic, pampering atmosphere underscored by Asian-themed furnishings and fabrics. Extensive use of crosscut travertine and Kalahari red marble (on the floor and in the shower) imbues the space with resort-style luxury.

Faux-bamboo cabinetry accommodates the two sinks, and Chinese benches hold towels and sundries at each end of the tub. Sheers printed with a Chinese-inspired medallion motif soften the window and doors, leaving the task of light control and privacy to Roman shades in gold and persimmon. Wall treatments add color and texture: The rust red window wall features a faux-grass-cloth paint treatment created by brushing the walls with a broom after the paint has been applied. The walls flanking the French doors and dressing table (see pages 186–187) feature a three-color Venetian plaster treatment that yields the look of alabaster.

ABOVE: A VANITY BUILT TO LOOK LIKE A BAMBOO DRESSER EXHIBITS METICULOUS ATTENTION TO DETAIL, WHICH EXTENDS TO THE LATTICE MOTIF UNDER THE SINK BASE. DESIGNING THE PIECE TO STAND ON LEGS WITH NO TOE-KICK ENHANCES THE ILLUSION OF CONVERTED FURNITURE.

OPPOSITE: MOSAICS OF TRAVERTINE AND RED KALAHARI MARBLE CREATE THE APPEARANCE OF LATTICEWORK IN THE LUXURIOUS SHOWER. THE BRUSHED-CHROME FIXTURES ECHO THE STAINLESS-STEEL STRIPS IN THE FLOOR. DESIGNED FOR TWO, THE SHOWER HAS A BUILT-IN SEAT AND SEVERAL SHOWER JETS.

OPPOSITE: KALAHARI MARBLE TOPS THE VANITIES, WHILE TRAVERTINE FRAMES THE MIRRORS. A CHINESE STOOL PROVIDES SEATING AT THE DRESSING TABLE. A THREE-COLOR VENETIAN PLASTER PAINT TREATMENT GIVES THE WALL DEPTH AND SUBTLE SHEEN.

ABOVE: THIS VANITY INCORPORATES A DRESSING TABLE THAT DROPS DOWN TO A CONVENIENT HEIGHT FOR SITTING.

Hidden Treasure

Underneath a historic townhouse in London's Kensington Square hides a gem of a bathroom that exudes whimsy and wit.

Left: Small mosaic tiles in shades of black, gray, and white form a classic scallop pattern in the shower.

Opposite: Recessed into a niche created for the vanity, a jeweled mirror hangs above a marble sink skirted with an antique Victorian veil from Morocco. The soffit at the top of the recess hides modern task lighting.

THE ARCHED OPEN
SHOWER TWINKLES
WITH EMBEDDED FIBER-
OPTIC LIGHTING. THE
SCONCE HUNG LOW ON
THE WALL BESIDE THE
SINK WAS ORIGINALLY A
DECORATIVE ITEM FROM
MARRAKECH. MOUNTED
TO THE WALL OVER A
LIGHTBULB, IT PROVIDES
DRAMATIC ACCENT
LIGHTING.

d

Down in the underbelly of this 17th-century home hides an
unexpected space of utter glamour and luxury. What had in
a previous life been a humble coal cellar has been reshaped
into a fantasy of jewellike accents and froths of lace.

Mixing the latest lighting techniques with decorative
antique fixtures allows the space to glow softly yet provides
illumination where needed. Electrified wall sconces were
fabricated from purely decorative objects picked up in
Marrakech; wiring and lightbulbs gave them a new function.

The cavernous arched shower is large enough to forgo
doors, yet it retains a feeling of intimacy with the use of
playful fiber-optic lighting that twinkles overhead like a
starry night sky.

Pitching the floor slightly toward the shower drain
eliminates the need for a curb to separate the stall from the
rest of the room. The unbroken floor space creates a more
expansive feeling in this subterranean room.

Draping the vanity in an antique Victorian veil gives it
the look of a dressing table while allowing it to retain the
function of a sink. If you look closely, the mosaic tiles show
through the lace, like the glimpse of lingerie.

OPPOSITE: MOSAIC TILES ADD AN ART DECO ACCENT TO THE RECESS, ENDOWING IT WITH A STRONGER VISUAL PRESENCE. FIBER-OPTIC LIGHTING SET IN A RANDOM PATTERN IN THE SHOWER CEILING TILES GIVES THE EFFECT OF A STAR-FILLED SKY, ADDING TO THE OVERALL MAGIC OF THIS UNEXPECTED ROOM. A MAMMOTH SHOWERHEAD SUPPLIES A CLOUDBURST OF WATER UNDER THE ARCHED CEILING.

ABOVE: A MIRROR-BACKED BOOKCASE CREATES OPENNESS IN A ROOM WITH NO WINDOWS. IT SHOWCASES DECORATIVE ITEMS AND THROWS AMBIENT LIGHT BACK INTO THE CHAMBER. THE SCONCES OVER THE CHAISE LONGUE MATCH THE PAIR FLANKING THE VANITY.

New Country Style 6

Modern Mediterranean

The saturated color of sunny tiles accented by dark wood evokes a Spanish influence.

Left: Simple carving and old brass hardware highlight the antique Moroccan console that now serves as a vanity.

Opposite: Custom-colored Mexican tile runs from floor to ceiling, around the tub, and into the shower. The ceiling beams, rediscovered when the 8-foot ceiling was removed, are stained deep brown to balance the dark floor.

RIGHT: A COUNTERTOP OF HONED FOSSIL STONE IN A DEEP MAHOGANY COLOR TOPS THIS MOROCCAN CHEST. OIL-RUBBED BRONZE FIXTURES AND SOAP DISPENSER SUIT THE RUSTIC CHARACTER OF THE FURNITURE PIECE AND FORM PART OF THE CHORUS OF DARK ACCENTS THAT CONTRAST WITH THE YELLOW TILE.

Enveloped in a sunny glow, this master bath combines ethnic and modern elements to create an updated interpretation of Mediterranean style. An antique Moroccan chest anchors the room and defines its ethnic accent. White oak floors treated to an ebonized finish ground the space. Beams rediscovered when the 8-foot ceiling was removed are stained a dark brown to match the rest of the woodwork.

To balance these dark tones, saturated, sunny yellow tile covers the walls from floor to ceiling and frames the tub. Clear glass encloses the shower stall to maximize the sense of space in the room. Although compact, the shower offers the luxury of a rain-shower head and a steam component. A transom window at the top provides ventilation to minimize mildew problems.

Accessory details contribute to the updated interpretation of traditional style. The mirror frames and étagère (see page 197), although stained a deep brown to match the floor and console, have sleek, modern lines. The barrel shades clipped onto the transitional-style bronze sconces also introduce a contemporary element. Although lampshades are a relatively minor aspect of the overall design, they can help set the tone of a scheme.

ABOVE: A RAIN-SHOWER HEAD AND STEAM COMPONENT PACK A LOT OF LUXURY INTO A SMALL SPACE. THE COMPACT SHOWER FEELS LARGER THAN ITS FOOTPRINT, THANKS TO CLEAR GLASS WALLS. A TRANSOM WINDOW AT THE TOP OF THE SHOWER DOOR PROVIDES VENTILATION.

ABOVE: TO USE ALL THE AVAILABLE SPACE, THE TUB DECKING EXTENDS INTO THE SHOWER STALL TO
CREATE A BENCH. MOUNTING THE TUB FAUCET ON THE SIDE WALL PRESERVES THE CLEAN LINES OF THE
TILED SURROUND.

Set
in Stone

In a fresh take on country French style, salvaged stone, limestone, and concrete bring a look of venerable antiquity to this bathroom.

Left: Rough-hewn beams with mortiselike cutouts define a freeform screen for one side of the open shower.

Opposite: A 17th-century French horse trough on salvaged stone supports serves as the bathroom sink. Tumbled-limestone pavers continue the color and texture of the sink across the floor. Ancient cisterns inspired the custom-designed gray concrete tub.

SET IN STONE

Stone gives this bathroom its aged, rustic character. Tumbled-limestone tiles define the wall and floor of the shower itself, and rough-textured limestone pavers cover the remaining floor area. Massive stone troughs imported from France serve as sinks, and the tub, formed from concrete, resembles a stone cistern. Bleached ceiling beams and plastered walls blend with the limestone and create an airy, open envelope of antique white.

The design of this large, octagonal master bath was inspired by European-style wetrooms, in which the shower area is open to the rest of the room. Although the look is streamlined and visually simple, it involves some special construction considerations. The whole room must be made watertight by laying a waterproof membrane under the floors and behind the walls. Because the entire floor is part of the shower, it must be raised to accommodate drainpipes and it must slope gently to facilitate drainage. Natural stone is the ideal nonskid material for the floor and imparts an aged, rough-hewn look that communicates country style.

Set in Stone

Below: An overscale mirror frame fashioned from distressed-tin panels balances the visual heft of the stone sink. Antique linen draperies can be drawn across the French doors for privacy. The fabric softens a room dominated by stone.

204

Above: Smaller floor tiles in the immediate shower area facilitate drainage. Hooks hold towels close enough to reach but far away enough to avoid getting splashed.

BELOW: THE ESSENCE OF COUNTRY STYLE IS TO
COMBINE FUNCTION WITH BEAUTY: HANDMADE
FRENCH SOAPS ARE WITHIN EASY REACH,
DISPLAYED IN A DISTRESSED WOODEN BOWL.

SET IN STONE

ABOVE: AN OVERSIZE OTTOMAN BUILT FROM MESQUITE AND UPHOLSTERED IN FRENCH QUILTS OFFERS A SOFT SPOT FOR LOUNGING.

Designed for Pampering

TRADITIONAL ARCHITECTURE PLUS RETRO FURNITURE
EQUALS A HIGH-STYLE SPA WITH ATTITUDE.

LEFT: EGG-SIZE ROCK
CRYSTALS DANGLING
FROM CURVING
WROUGHT-IRON
ARMS GLAMORIZE
THIS ELECTRIFIED
ANTIQUE
CHANDELIER.

OPPOSITE: THE USE
OF IRON—IN THE
CHANDELIER, THE
EXTERIOR CARRIAGE
SCONCE, AND THE
GARDEN CHAIR—
CREATES CONTINUITY
BETWEEN INDOORS
AND OUT.

DESIGNED FOR PAMPERING

INSTEAD OF THE USUAL NONFLAMMABLE LOGS, THIS GAS FIREPLACE HOLDS A PYRAMID OF STONE BALLS. HONED MARBLE FLOORING GIVES AN OLDER LOOK THAN POLISHED STONE DOES, AND IT'S A SAFER, NONSLIP SURFACE. THIN STRIPS OF THE SAME MARBLE ACCENT THE WAINSCOTING AS A LINER TILE, UNIFYING THE WALLS AND FLOOR.

Traditional architectural features and materials give the impression that this bathroom originally served as something else—a sitting room, perhaps, or a bedroom. But it's all new, designed specifically to celebrate bathing as pampering pleasure. The gas fireplace provides warmth, atmosphere, and soft lighting. The marble-clad tub, positioned between the fireplace and French doors to the terrace, invites the bather to enjoy both the flickering flames and the garden landscape while indulging in a long soak.

A wainscoting of white subway tile wraps the walls, making a clean, vintage-feeling background for the marble. Beveled-edge mirrors in white frames hang above the wainscoting all around the room, reflecting light and views and creating an illusion of transparency.

The shower and toilet each have a separate compartment hidden behind mirrored, multipane doors (see page 215). Tucking them out of sight enhances the spalike quality of the room. A pair of 1950s chairs and a 1960s coffee table, placed to encourage relaxation, contrast with the marble and tile surroundings for a sophisticated style statement.

Rough marble floors and antique chestnut beams in the cathedral ceiling add a rustic note. Along with the traditional architecture, they anchor the room with a feeling of timelessness and longevity.

ABOVE: A SMALL FLAT-SCREEN TV HANGS HIGH IN THE CORNER FOR EASY VIEWING WHILE SOAKING. DEEP BASEBOARDS AND TRADITIONAL MOLDINGS ANCHOR THE ARCHITECTURAL STYLE IN THE PAST.

OPPOSITE: A MARBLE-TOP CONSOLE SINK STANDS ON CRYSTAL-AND-METAL LEGS FOR A CONTEMPORARY STYLE STATEMENT. THE EXPOSED TRAP MATCHES THE COLOR AND FINISH OF THE FAUCETS, SCONCES, AND TOWEL BARS TO CREATE A UNIFIED APPEARANCE.

OPPOSITE: SETTING THE TUB PERPENDICULAR TO THE WALL ENABLES THE BATHER TO VIEW BOTH THE FIREPLACE AND THE GARDEN. UNEXPECTED ACCENTS, SUCH AS THE RETRO RED CHAIRS, UPDATE THE SPACE, ADDING AN URBAN-CHIC FLAVOR TO A COUNTRY BATH.

ABOVE: BUILT-IN LINEN CABINETS IN THE VESTIBULE MIMIC FURNITURE. BEHIND MIRRORED, MULTIPANE DOORS ARE THE STEAM SHOWER (ON THE LEFT) AND THE TOILET (ON THE RIGHT). THE COMPARTMENTS ARE BUILT AS BOXES SET INTO THE OPEN TWO-STORY SPACE.

New Country Charm

Contemporary ebony framing around farmhouse-style bathroom fixtures puts a new twist on a comfortable vintage look.

Left: A farmhouse sink on an ebony stand blends contemporary and traditional styles. Because the sink has a relatively narrow rim, the wall behind is built out to provide shelf space.

Opposite: A glass block window set into the wall between the sink and shower allows the exchange of light between the two spaces. The mosaic tile used in the shower is incorporated into the border of the floor in the sitting/bathing area.

A growing trend in master suite design is to incorporate the bathroom and the bedroom in one large space. Ironically, this new twist on the bed/bath floor plan is actually reviving an arrangement from the past, before indoor plumbing made separate bathrooms a standard feature. Washstands with pretty bowls and pitchers were customary items of bedroom furniture, and in wealthier households, copper tubs set up in bedrooms were filled with buckets of warm water carried up by the maids.

In this large, second-story master suite, massive farmhouse sinks on contemporary ebony stands replace the washstand, and a capacious and graceful porcelain tub updates the old copper model. Thanks to plumbing, this modern take on one-room living is convenient and even luxuriously indulgent. The sinks and tub align on the exterior wall, where a shallow, tiled bumpout contains the plumbing lines. A pair of upholstered chairs with French legs and classic styling takes the functional edge off the space. For the sake of practicality, tile covers the floor at the bath end (wood floors define the sleeping area, not shown). A wide band of smaller mosaic tiles trims the larger tile, creating the look of a rug.

Small-Space Elegance

ACCESS TO THE OUTDOORS MAKES A SMALL
BATH SEEM LARGER AND ENDOWS IT WITH THE
FEELING OF A WEEKEND COUNTRY RETREAT.

LEFT: A MIRRORED
BACK INSIDE THE
MEDICINE CABINET
AIDS IN FINDING
BOTTLES HIDDEN
BEHIND TALLER
NEIGHBORS. A
VINTAGE-STYLE
WALLMOUNT SOAP
AND CUP HOLDER
KEEPS THE SINK TIDY.

OPPOSITE: SHELVES
SET BETWEEN
THE WALL STUDS
ON EACH SIDE OF
THE SINK PROVIDE
DISPLAY SPACE
FOR COLLECTIONS
AND TOILETRIES. A
BAMBOO STORAGE
PIECE SUBSTITUTES
FOR TRADITIONAL
CABINETRY.

Tucked under the eaves, this modest bathroom offers all the amenities with stylish country charm. Instead of tile wainscoting, a chair rail and picture-frame molding give the lower walls the appearance of paneling. This is a simple and inexpensive way to give walls a high-end look. The moldings are applied to the flat wall; painting the wall and moldings the same color enhances the illusion of paneling. Above the chair rail, a striped wallpaper makes the ceiling feel higher—a useful trick, particularly over the tub, where the pitch is lowest. Behind the sink, the chair rail molding is replaced with a tile edge, and the wall is painted for a more waterproof surface.

Small hexagon tiles on the floor evoke the same vintage style as the pedestal sink and footed tub. The simple white tiles run wall to wall without any decorative borders. This simplicity helps keep the room feeling open and uncluttered.

Another architectural trick endows the sink wall with interesting detail. Building out the wall 2 inches creates a niche that visually groups together the medicine cabinet and its two flanking shelf areas. Contrasting paint emphasizes the mirror section as the room's focal point.

Through the Garden Gate

ONCE A SUNROOM, NOW A BATHROOM, THIS SPACE OFFERS A FRESH TAKE ON COTTAGE STYLE.

LEFT: AN ARCHED BACKSPLASH ECHOES THE CURVE MOTIF OF THE WAINSCOTING AND HAS A PRACTICAL ASPECT TOO, PROTECTING THE WALL FROM SPLASHES.

OPPOSITE: SHAPED LIKE A GARDEN GATE, BEADED-BOARD WAINSCOTING FLANKS THE SHOWER ENTRANCE. THE FRAMELESS GLASS SHOWER DOOR PRACTICALLY DISAPPEARS, SHOWCASING THE BRICKLIKE WALL BEYOND.

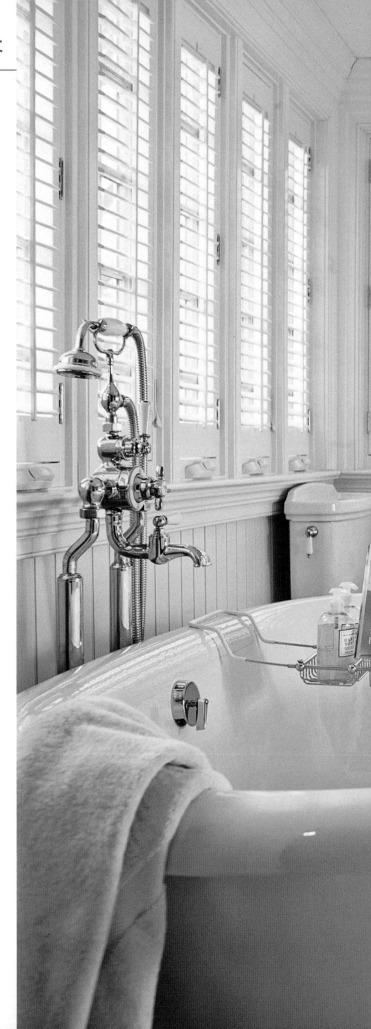

ALTHOUGH THE FLOOR IS MADE FROM POLISHED STONE, THE SMALL TILES PREVENT EXCESSIVE SLIPPERINESS: THE GROUT LINES BETWEEN THEM ACT AS A BRAKE IF YOU START TO SLIP. METAL CLIPS HOLD THE BEVELED-EDGE MIRROR ON THE WALL. ITS PLAIN METAL FRAME MATCHES THE SHINY CHROME OF THE FAUCETS, TUB FILLER, AND VANITY PULLS FOR A UNIFIED EFFECT. THE TOILET TANK HAS A LOW BACKSPLASH TO KEEP ITEMS FROM FALLING BEHIND THE TOILET.

Carved out of an existing sunporch, this bathroom enjoys an extraordinary amount of light, thanks to the original casement windows. Interior shutters provide light control and privacy. Installed to clear the casement cranks, the shutters can stay in place whether windows are open or closed.

Shutters and beaded-board wainscoting suggest cottage style, and the furniture-style vanities and freestanding tub reinforce the look. The shower wall, however, takes the cottage motif to the level of elegance, playing on the garden-inspired aspect of cottage style (see page 225). Instead of continuing along the usual horizontal line, the wainscoting on each side of the shower door curves to resemble a garden gate. The doorway frames the shower wall, which is tiled with 3×6-inch red tiles to resemble a brick wall.

The shower door opening is tall enough for its framing to fall just under the crown molding, so the crown is framed out and mitered around the door casing. This creates a more stylish header and adds visual importance to the shower entrance.

Roughing It in Style

MARINE FINISHES AND COASTAL MATERIALS STAMP
THIS BATH WITH DISTINCTIVE RUSTIC CHARACTER.

LEFT: THE SHOWER
CEILING IS CLAD IN
CEDAR AND THE
WINDOW CASING
IN MAHOGANY,
TWO WOODS THAT
NATURALLY REPEL
WATER. SECTIONS OF
CROSSCUT BEACH
STONE SET INTO THE
STONE FLOOR IN A
RANDOM PATTERN
GIVE A NOD TO THE
NEARBY OCEAN.

OPPOSITE: TUCKED
IN THE CORNER, A
SOAKING TUB TAKES
ADVANTAGE OF THE
VIEW. BEADED-
BOARD PANELING
AND GREEN GLASS
KNOBS ON THE
CABINETRY EVOKE
COTTAGE STYLE.

RIGHT: A HONED GRANITE COUNTERTOP OFFERS A MORE RUSTIC LOOK THAN POLISHED STONE. THE TWO MEDICINE CABINETS REST ON A SHELF, CREATING A THIRD NICHE BETWEEN THEM FOR TOILETRY STORAGE. BEYOND THE FREESTANDING VANITY IS THE DOOR TO THE SEPARATE TOILET COMPARTMENT.

How do you break up a room for privacy yet keep the feeling open and airy? This bath solves the dilemma by installing an island for the twin vanities in the middle of the room. Two salvaged porch posts flank the island, connected by a shelf that supports the medicine cabinets. Latticework hung from the ceiling helps anchor the cabinets in place. This arrangement blocks sight lines, hiding the tub and shower, but allows views out the windows.

The beaded-board wainscoting continues on the back of the island, connecting it visually to the walls, while the lattice framing for the hanging cabinets allows air to circulate in the room.

Instead of being tiled, the shower walls are covered with a white gypsum cement usually used for crafts projects; the gypsum cement is coated with several layers of acrylic marine paint. This finish forms a watertight seal and a smooth surface. The paint's water-repellent properties allow a large window to be installed in the shower without any concern about the effect of moisture on the frame.

OPPOSITE: THE VIEW FROM THE MASTER BEDROOM SHOWS THE EXPOSED CEILING RAFTERS AND LOFTY CEILING OF THE BATHROOM. PAINTED BEADED BOARD FINISHES THE BACKS OF THE VANITY AND MEDICINE CABINETS, UNITING THEM WITH THE WAINSCOTING AROUND THE ROOM.

Rock of Ages

MATERIALS OF VARYING AGES GATHERED FROM AROUND THE WORLD PRODUCE A UNIQUE BATH THAT REFLECTS THE LOCAL ATMOSPHERE.

LEFT: OIL-RUBBED BRONZE FAUCETS HAVE A "LIVE FINISH"— IT WEARS OFF OVER TIME. THIS RESULTS IN A GENUINELY WORN LOOK BECAUSE THE METAL UNDERNEATH SHOWS THROUGH AND TARNISHES.

OPPOSITE: THE BOLD COLOR AND PATTERN OF SLATE FROM CHINA RESEMBLES A MURAL SPREAD OVER THE TUB AND FLOOR. A CHINESE GRANITE BOULDER SLICED IN HALF AND POLISHED INSIDE CREATES A PAIR OF SINKS FOR MATCHING VANITIES.

THE VANITIES AND LOUVERED CLOSET DOOR ARE MADE FROM MESQUITE BOARDS SALVAGED FROM OLD DOORS AND GATES. (MESQUITE IS AN ENDANGERED SPECIES AND CAN NO LONGER BE CUT IN MEXICO.) ITALIAN SCONCES WITH HANDBLOWN GLASS SHADES MOUNTED ON WROUGHT-IRON FIXTURES FLANK THE MIRROR.

Country style in Sonoma, California, is expressed with organic shapes and natural finishes. The irony is that in this homespun bath, most of the materials come from outside the United States. The slate floor and wall tiles are imported from China; so are the green granite sinks. The sconces came from Italy, and the custom vanities were made in Mexico. This is country style with a global flavor.

Recycled materials add vintage character. The cabinets are crafted from mesquite culled from old doors or gates found south of the border. The toasty color results from bleaching the wood; its natural color is quite dark. Salvaged rusty painted ceiling tiles have been fashioned into mirror frames that hang over each sink.

The walls are finished with base-coat plaster, which is usually used as an undercoat. Tinted with an oatmeal-color pigment added to the plaster before it's applied, the material gives an earthy, unpolished finish to the room.

A glass splash guard encloses a portion of the tub (see page 233), protecting the floor and vanity while preserving the open look. A fabric panel hung from a short wallmount rod adds soft texture to balance all the rough, hard surfaces in the room.

Fresh & White

A CRISP WHITE BATH CREATES A FRAMEWORK FOR OCEAN VIEWS, INSTILLING A FEELING OF SERENITY IN THIS VINTAGE COTTAGE SPACE.

LEFT: CUT CRYSTALS ON THE CHANDELIER, PLACED UNDER CEILING WINDOWS, ADD MORE GLITTER TO THE SPARKLE OF THIS ROOM.

OPPOSITE: AIRY CAFE CURTAINS SCREEN THE LOWER PART OF THE WINDOW WHILE LIGHT ENTERS UNOBSTRUCTED THROUGH THE TOP HALF OF THE GLASS. THE FREESTANDING TUB ON ITS PEDESTAL BASE MAKES A COUNTRY-COTTAGE STYLE STATEMENT.

ADDING A FLIRTY SKIRT
TO THE SINK CABINET
BRINGS COUNTRY CHARM
AND SOFTNESS TO WHAT
IS OFTEN A HARD-EDGED
SPACE. A WALLMOUNT
MAGNIFYING MIRROR
SUPPLEMENTS THE
OVERSINK MIRROR FOR
GROOMING TASKS.

Venetian mirrors add instant glamour to an otherwise humble space. When paired with polished silver and nickel-plated fixtures, they introduce a rich sparkle that supplies an elegant foil to a simple white bath. The addition of the softest blush of lavender on the walls accentuates the purity of the white fixtures and tile, actually making the white seem whiter.

Glass doors on the cabinetry display the pretty items stored within. And because the sight lines continue through to the back of the cabinet, the room feels larger.

Blond wood flooring adds visual warmth to keep the white and pale lavender room from feeling sterile. This delicate balance of clean lines with cool colors and warm wood results in a charming room with a country sensibility.

239

LEFT: A DEEP BENCH IN THE SHOWER SUPPLIES A PLACE TO SIT AS WELL AS A SURFACE FOR NEEDED SUPPLIES. THE FRAMELESS ENCLOSURE WAS CUT TO FIT THE PROFILE OF THE TILED SEAT, LIMITING THE NUMBER OF VERTICAL LINES IN THE GLASS. THIS KEEPS THE LOOK UNCLUTTERED.

ABOVE: FOR A CLASSIC LOOK, A FLOOR-MOUNTED TUB FILLER IS INSTALLED BETWEEN THE SIDE OF THE TUB AND THE WALL. POLISHED CHROME GIVES A SPARKLE THAT IS REPEATED IN THE VENETIAN MIRRORS.

Contemporary Comfort

7

Minimalism in a Richer Key

RUGGED STONE MAKES A STUNNING BACKDROP FOR SLEEK FIXTURES AND CONTEMPORARY BATH FITTINGS.

LEFT: CHINESE SLATE, CHOSEN FOR ITS RUGGED TEXTURE AND FLECKED SURFACE, COVERS THE FLOOR IN TWO SIZES OF TILE.

OPPOSITE: MOUNTING THE PLUMBING ON THE WALL RATHER THAN AT THE END OF THE TUB CREATES AN UNOBSTRUCTED VIEW OF THE WILDERNESS LANDSCAPE. THE CLEAN LINES OF THE CONTEMPORARY FAUCETS WORK AS A DESIGN FOIL FOR THE RUSTICITY OF THE SLATE WALL.

MINIMALISM IN A RICHER KEY

FRAMED AGAINST A
DRAMATIC WALL OF
ROUGH SLATE, THE
ASYMMETRICAL TUB
LOOKS LIKE A PIECE
OF SCULPTURE. LIGHT
COMING IN THROUGH
FLOOR-TO-CEILING
WINDOWS THROWS THE
CRAGGY SURFACES
INTO HIGH RELIEF,
ACCENTUATING THE
STONE'S NATURAL
BEAUTY.

This minimalist design approach makes the materials the stars of the bathroom. Rough-hewn Chinese slate in three sizes and textures covers the walls and floor. The wall slabs have the roughest texture, showcasing the characteristic flaked and uneven surface. On the floor, rough pavers define the tub area, while larger, smoother rectangles cover the remaining floor. The shower stall is clad in smooth Brazilian slate, a more practical application because the surface is easier to keep clean.

The cabinets (see pages 248–249) are fabricated out of salvaged steel found at an industrial materials supplier. The metal had been used as plate steel that was laid over potholes in the road and had rusted into a cratered finish. Cleaned up, the aged surfaces turned out to be texturally interesting and a wonderfully unusual addition to the bath.

Above the sink, a hopper window takes the place of a mirror. These windows hinge at the bottom and tilt into the room, encouraging air circulation and offering a view. For makeup application, a separate dressing table area is set to the right of one sink; a corresponding shaving area is across the room.

MINIMALISM IN A RICHER KEY

RIGHT: COUNTERTOPS FABRICATED FROM
WENGE, A NATURALLY DARK AFRICAN WOOD,
PICK UP THE SMOKY TONES OF THE STEEL
VANITY FRAME. THE WINDOWS FLANKING
THE TUB WERE SET AT THE TOP OF THE
SUBFLOORING, EXTENDING BELOW THE
FINISHED LEVEL TO CREATE THE LOOK OF A
GLASS WALL.

BELOW: SMOOTH BRAZILIAN SLATE COVERS
THE INSIDE OF THE STEAM SHOWER STALL.
BEING A LESS POROUS MATERIAL THAN THE
CHINESE SLATE, IT WORKS BETTER IN A HIGH-
MOISTURE LOCATION.

Girl with the Pearl

WHITE SURROUNDINGS AND LIGHT WOODTONES
KEEP THE ATTENTION FOCUSED ON THE ROOM'S
STUNNING ARTWORK, AN HOMAGE TO VERMEER.

LEFT: THE MARBLED
NICHE BETWEEN THE
TOILET AND SHOWER
PROVIDES A SPOT
FOR THE DRESSING
TABLE. COVERING
THE TABLETOP WITH
GLASS KEEPS THE
WOOD LOOKING
PRISTINE.

OPPOSITE: FRENCH
DOORS LEAD INTO
THE NEW BATHROOM
SO THAT EVEN WHEN
THE DOORS ARE
CLOSED, THE MURAL
IS VISIBLE FROM THE
MASTER BEDROOM
AND HALL.

GIRL WITH THE PEARL

TEMPERED-GLASS
DOORS SEPARATE THE
TOILET CLOSET FROM
THE BATHING AREA.
THE USE OF GLASS
PERMITS THE LIGHT
FROM THE SKYLIGHTS
IN BOTH WATER CLOSET
AND SHOWER TO FLOW
INTO THE REST OF THE
BATHROOM.

The decision to fill in two windows and cover the entire wall with a mural drove all of the other design decisions in this bathroom. The stunning interpretation of Jan Vermeer's 17th-century painting popularly known as *Girl with a Pearl Earring* dominates the bathroom as well as the view from the bedroom and hall. To give it pride of place, the rest of the room is quiet, elegant, and understated.

White Carrara marble covers the floors and encloses the shower and toilet compartments. The tub surround, vanity, and dressing table are built from golden quartersawn ash. The pale palette enhances the light coming from a large south-facing window and imbues the room with an open, airy feeling.

To enhance that openness, the whirlpool tub and double-sink vanity float in the center of the room, separated by a marble-clad partial wall (see page 255). The dressing table takes advantage of a nook between the shower and toilet compartments; the sleek modern chair and light fixture blend with the gray-veined marble rather than calling attention to themselves.

BELOW: LARGE PANELS OF CARRARA MARBLE COVER THE FLOORS AND WALLS OF THE BATHROOM, INCLUDING THE SHOWER.

ABOVE: MOUNTED ON THE PARTIAL WALL THAT SEPARATES THE VANITY AND THE TUB, THE STREAMLINED FAUCET IS UNDERSTATED AND CONTEMPORARY. A MARBLE COUNTERTOP AND UNDERMOUNTED SINKS MATCH THE CLEAN LINES OF THE VANITY.

OPPOSITE: THE TUB AND SINKS WERE SET BACK-TO-BACK TO FLOAT IN THE MIDDLE OF THE ROOM. THE HALF-WALL CREATES A BACKSPLASH AND PROVIDES A WAY TO HIDE THE PLUMBING PIPES. THE MURAL WAS PAINTED ON CANVAS SO IT CAN BE TAKEN DOWN IF THE OWNERS DECIDE TO MOVE.

Dramatic Framing

Industrial materials form a striking bath that blends loftlike sensibilities with an atmosphere of warmth.

Left: Frosted glass set into milled-steel frames defines the walls and doors of the bathroom.

Opposite: Tubular sconces mounted on the mirror provide lighting at the sinks. Kasota stone was used for the counter because of its warm tones, which work well with the Douglas fir drawers and flooring.

Dramatic Framing

Right: Closet shelving, drawers, and rods are all adjustable, allowing different setups for changing needs. Track lighting accommodates any alteration. Raising the drawers off the floor leaves space for shoes.

Below right: Encased in frosted glass, the bathroom divides the bedroom from the study. The wood panels opposite the vanity hide shallow storage for medicines and toiletries.

A Minneapolis loft in winter could be stark and cold, but this bath remains cozy, thanks to an ingenious grille of large radiator pipes mounted in front of the expansive windows. The pipes radiate warmth into the room and create an interesting effect for the window treatment. The great benefit of radiators is that they continue to emit heat after the furnace shuts off, supplying a more even type of warmth than forced hot air.

Frosted glass set in frames of mill-finished steel divides the bath and closet from the rest of the raw, open space. The materials suit the industrial ambience of loft living while supplying light-filled privacy.

Because the vanity stands in front of an exterior wall, its mirror was mounted on additional metal framing and raised above the counter by several inches to allow more daylight into the sink area.

To achieve the look of wallmount faucets in the absence of a wall on which to mount them, the designers used restaurant-style kitchen fixtures. They were extended higher on longer legs to work with the vessel sinks set on the countertop.

Opposite: The mill-finished steel used throughout the bathroom is repeated in the vanity, furnishing its legs and frame as well as providing bars for hand towels. The radiator grille over the windows is visible in the background.

Tropical Breezes

ASIAN TOUCHES AND TWO KINDS OF TUBS CREATE AN OASIS OF SENSUALITY IN A RETREAT DESIGNED FOR RELAXING.

LEFT: ART GLASS TILE MOSAICS IN A BASKET-WEAVE PATTERN CONTINUE THE WOVEN THEME FROM THE GRASS-CLOTH WALLCOVERING.

OPPOSITE: THE SHOWER FLOOR AND WALLS ARE SOLID-SURFACING MATERIAL, ROUTERED FOR SAFETY AND APPEARANCE. A PIECE OF WATERPROOF ART DRESSES UP THE STALL IN AN UNEXPECTED WAY.

THE LANAI OFF THE
MASTER BATH HOLDS
A JETTED SOAKING
TUB. THE WIDE SOLID-
SURFACING DECK
ACCOMMODATES MOOD-
SETTING CANDLES AND
PLANTS AS WELL AS
BEVERAGE GLASSES.
THE CARVED SCREEN
ON THE WALL ADDS A
POLYNESIAN ELEMENT.

Designed as a personal sanctuary to promote soothing relaxation, this master bath/spa suite boasts two tubs: a jetted tub on the lanai, or veranda, and a hand-hammered copper tub in the adjoining bathroom. Dark hardwood floors, grass-cloth wallcovering, cabinet doors with rattan insets, and wall panels with glass tiles in a woven pattern combine to imbue the space with a tropical-island air. As might befit a tropical dwelling, the lanai, bathroom, and bedroom open into each other through wide doorways that enhance the breezy feeling.

In the bathroom, the sinks lie on opposite sides of the room, each with its own built-in furniture-style cupboard and television. (The televisions are equally visible from the tub, so theoretically you could share the bath with a friend and each watch a different program.)

Instead of moldings, wide planks of quartersawn oak stained dark red-brown outline the doors, windows, and walls, creating a dramatic contrast with the grass-cloth walls. The effect resembles that of shoji screens and continues in a striking mural set behind the copper tub (see page 264).

Designed as functional art, the copper tub has double walls to insulate against the loss of heat. This allows for extended soaks while daydreaming about Tahiti.

ABOVE: SOLID SURFACING IS USED FOR THE COUNTERTOP AND CONTINUES UP THE WALL, WHERE IT HAS BEEN SCORED INTO 16-INCH SQUARES TO MIMIC THE LOOK OF TILE. A WALL OF CABINETRY BUILT OPPOSITE THE TUB PROVIDES A SPACE TO SET THE TV, ENCOURAGING LONG, RELAXING SOAKS.

RIGHT: HAMMERED COPPER GIVES THE SINK A HANDCRAFTED APPEAL, APPEARING EXOTIC BUT HUMBLE. THE OIL-BRONZED FAUCET AND SPIGOTS HARMONIZE WITH THE WOODWORK.

OPPOSITE: A CUSTOM GLASS TILE MOSAIC TRIPTYCH MAKES A STUNNING BACKDROP FOR THE HAMMERED COPPER TUB. THE LOW LUSTER OF OIL-RUBBED BRONZE PLUMBING BLENDS WITH THE DARK-STAINED WOOD FRAME.

Two for One

A SHARED SHOWER CREATES THE IMPRESSION
OF TWO SEPARATE BATHROOMS, PROVIDING
THE LUXURY OF A DOUBLE MASTER BATH.

LEFT: A CIRCULAR MEDICINE CABINET SUGGESTS A PORTHOLE (OR A GIANT ASPIRIN). SIMPLE GEOMETRIC SHAPES PROVIDE A COUNTERPOINT TO THE JIGSAW-PUZZLE EFFECT OF THE TILED WALLS.

OPPOSITE: BLACK, BROWN, AND SILVER MOSAIC TILES OF VARYING SIZES FORM A STRIKING BACKDROP FOR A CONTEMPORARY SINK. THE SILVER TILES REFLECT THE TONES OF THE NICKEL FIXTURES.

Two for One

BLACK AND WHITE TILE CONTINUES FROM ONE HALF OF THE BATH THROUGH THE SHARED SHOWER AND ONTO THE FLOOR OF THE OTHER HALF. WHITE WALLS DISTINGUISH THIS HALF OF THE BATH AS A SEPARATE AREA.

Separate bathrooms are an unrealized fantasy for many couples. If you have limited space and are willing to approach the problem from an unusual perspective, this may be the solution for your dream: Dispense with a tub and position the shower stall in the middle of the space. Make it accessible from both sides and devote the area on each side to a separate toilet and sink. Because the shower stall here is so large, glass walls and doors are not necessary, allowing the two sections of the bath to remain visible to each other, with a friendly border that allows each side to stay autonomous.

While matching sinks tie the two areas together, the tile from the shower continues onto the wall of one section, visually separating it from the all-white walls of the other section. The irregular tile layout produces a lively pattern. The sharp contrast of white fixtures against dark tile walls creates a dramatic effect and gives the eye a place to rest.

Zen
Retreat

ASIAN SIMPLICITY COMES TO FRUITION IN THIS
SOUTHERN CALIFORNIA HOME, PROVING THAT
OPULENCE CAN BE WROUGHT FROM HUMBLE MATERIALS.

LEFT: THE DULL FINISH AND DARK COLOR OF OIL-RUBBED BRONZE FIXTURES AND A VESSEL SINK ACCENT THE WARM REDDISH HUES OF THE CEDAR WALLS AND SLATTED TEAK COUNTER.

OPPOSITE: A JAPANESE SOAKING TUB CRAFTED FROM PORT ORFORD CEDAR (ALSO CALLED FINE-GRAINED HINOKI) RESTS ON A SLATTED TEAK FLOOR THAT ALLOWS FOR DRAINAGE AND CONVEYS AN ASIAN AESTHETIC.

ZEN RETREAT

Adjoining a guest room that also serves as an exercise gym, this bath has to accommodate multiple needs. Designed as a Japanese soaking bath, the space evokes an upscale Asian spa with a view of nature beyond the windows.

Slate tiles on the floor and walls resist moisture and create a subdued ambience conducive to relaxation. Cedar, redwood, mahogany, and teak have been thoughtfully deployed for the beauty of their colors and textures and for their resistance to humidity and water.

The slatted teak countertop echoes the flooring beside the tub; on the floor the slats hide drainage for potential splashes and overflows. A step for the tub (barely visible at the edge of the tub) also features teak slats. With a tub this deep, a step is essential.

To preserve the warm, dark color scheme, the toilet is dark gray rather than the more typical white. Even the faucets are dark in tone, fabricated from oil-rubbed bronze. This allows the soaking tub to stand out by contrast as the natural focal point.

Clean & Contemporary

A COMBINATION OF STONE, WOOD, AND BRUSHED
METAL BRINGS A SLEEK, UNCLUTTERED
AESTHETIC TO A CONTEMPORARY BATHROOM.

LEFT: VISIBLE IN THE MIRROR, THE CEILING SOFFIT DEFINES THE BATHROOM AS A MORE INTIMATE SPACE WITHIN AN OPEN FLOOR PLAN.

OPPOSITE: THE ORGANIC SHAPE OF THE BRUSHED STAINLESS-STEEL TUB STANDS IN CONTRAST TO THE STRAIGHT LINES THAT DOMINATE THE BATHROOM. A TUB LIKE THIS REQUIRES A STEP STOOL FOR SAFE ACCESS.

THE SOFFIT INSTALLED UNDER THE CATHEDRAL CEILING FURNISHES THE SHOWER AND TUB AREA WITH A SURFACE FOR INSTALLING DOWNLIGHTING. IN A HIGH-MOISTURE AREA, FIXTURES MUST BE SEALED; THESE ARE TRIMMED TO MATCH THE TUB FINISH. A SLIDING FROSTED-GLASS DOOR ENCLOSES THE TOILET AREA, PROVIDING PRIVACY WITHOUT BLOCKING LIGHT.

What could be more opulent than a custom-designed stainless-steel spa? This gleaming beauty was fabricated to the designer's specifications and built with a 4½-inch-thick insulated wall that improves heat retention and muffles the noise of water filling the tub.

In contrast to the industrial nature of the tub material, the vanity and storage cabinets are constructed of sen wood. Often called Japanese ash, it's actually a member of the ginseng family and is available in the United States primarily as a veneer. To create a strong design accent, the vanity's drawers are stained ebony, providing the look of two woods for the price of one.

The stone used in the shower is a type of quartzite, which is sandstone that has been subjected to immense heat and pressure through geological activity. Although traces of cross-bedding, or layers of sand laid down over millenia, may be preserved, fossils usually are not; however, minerals within the rock may form fernlike shapes that resemble fossils. The stone has a tough, moisture-resistant surface well-suited to shower installations.

The stall has two showerheads for the ultimate in self-indulgence: an overhead rain nozzle that creates the effect of a tropical deluge and another mounted on the wall for a more directed spray.

ABOVE: THE COLORS AND PATTERNS IN FOSSIL STONE CREATE AN ABSTRACT PATTERN WITH ABUNDANT NATURAL VARIETY. A CORNER SHELF CUT FROM A SLAB OF THE STONE KEEPS BATHING SUPPLIES HANDY. THE CLERESTORY WINDOW ADMITS NATURAL LIGHT AND PROVIDES VENTILATION.

OPPOSITE: THE LINEAR PATTERN IN THE WOOD VENEER UNDERSCORES THE CLEAN LINES OF THE ARCHITECTURE. THE OPEN VANITY OFFERS ROOMY STORAGE FOR TOILETRIES AND TOWELS; BASKETS AND METAL CONTAINERS KEEP THINGS TIDY. THE MIRROR IS RECESSED INTO THE WALL, BECOMING PART OF THE ARCHITECTURE INSTEAD OF SIMPLY A DECORATIVE ELEMENT.

Thinking of Asia

Chinese and Japanese motifs define the room's style, while a limited palette of materials infuses the space with the essence of peace and calm.

Left: A sleek gooseneck faucet suits the proportions of a deep custom-designed sink.

Opposite: Double sinks set back-to-back form an island in the room. The pagoda-inspired shape of the shared mirror and its decorative panel of burled ash evoke Chinese design. Vertical lighting strips embedded in the sides wash the mirror with light.

THE JAPANESE-STYLE
SOAKING TUB IS CLAD IN
THE SAME LIMESTONE
TILE USED THROUGHOUT
THE ROOM. FOR ADDED
COMFORT, RADIANT
HEAT WAS INSTALLED
UNDER THE NEW STONE
FLOORING. A VERTICAL
GRAB BAR ON THE
WALL ADJACENT TO THE
WINDOW DISCREETLY
PROVIDES FOR SAFETY.

Influences from Asia meld beautifully with contemporary design choices. Clean lines and a limited palette of materials—limestone, tile, rice paper, and mahogany—simplify the visual elements in the space and evoke a restful atmosphere. Limestone tiles on the floor, sinks, and Japanese-style soaking tub partner with faux-linen wall tiles in a similar color to create a luminous, light-filled space. Mahogany provides rich, warm contrast to the cool stone.

The Asian design theme is evident in the double lavatory, which stands in the center of the room, apparently free-floating and not tethered by its plumbing. (An unobtrusive central column contains the pipes, which come up from the floor.) The upturned arch of the double-sided mahogany-framed mirror recalls the roofline of a pagoda, while the shaped legs reflect Japanese influence. The same mahogany panels a wall of custom cabinets. To create the look of shoji screens on the upper cabinet doors, the recessed wood panels are covered with laminated rice paper.

Soaked in Simplicity

INSPIRED BY THE CLEAN LOOK OF CONTEMPORARY
SCANDINAVIAN DESIGN, AN OUTDATED RANCH HOUSE
GETS A MAKEOVER WITH WHITE WALLS AND BLOND WOOD.

LEFT: AN OPEN
CABINET AT ONE END
OF THE TUB MAKES A
DECORATIVE VIRTUE
OF STORAGE.

OPPOSITE: AN
OVERFLOWING
WHIRLPOOL BATH
RECIRCULATES
EXCESS WATER.
THE POINT OF
THESE TUBS IS TO
FILL THEM FULL
ENOUGH TO HAVE A
SLOW, CONTINUOUS
SPILLING OF WATER
OVER ALL SIDES
OF THE INNER
EDGES, ADDING
TO THE RELAXING
EXPERIENCE.

RIGHT: THE
WALKTHROUGH
SHOWER STALL
OCCUPIES A LONG,
NARROW SPACE
BETWEEN THE MASTER
BEDROOM AND THE
DOUBLE VANITIES ON
THE OTHER SIDE OF
THE WALL. A TRIANGLE
OF CARRARA MARBLE
FITS INTO THE CORNER
AS SHELVING.

Choosing a region for design inspiration can make the creative wheels turn in a way that triggers new approaches to existing situations. Scandinavian style in the past century has become identified with the look of clean white walls, simple honest stone, and unadorned blond wood. Applying these elements to this renovated bathroom infuses the existing space with a fresh new style.

The wall behind the pair of sinks stops short of the ceiling, allowing air to circulate freely around the room. This helps minimize mildew problems and allows light to bounce off the ceiling into both the lavatory area and the walkthrough shower on the other side of the partial wall. To allow more ambient light into the shower area, the wall shared with the master bedroom is pierced with frosted-glass windows.

Task lights on low-voltage cables run along the base of the ceiling beam to illuminate the vanity area. The swivel heads allow the direction of light to be angled as needed.

OPPOSITE: SHELLACKED WITH A TOUCH
OF AMBER FOR RICHER COLOR, A MAPLE
FARMHOUSE-STYLE TABLE PROVIDES
COUNTERSPACE FOR LARGE, SHALLOW
MARBLE SINKS. METAL RODS INSTALLED AS
STRETCHERS SERVE AS TOWEL BARS, AND
A CARRARA MARBLE SHELF BELOW OFFERS
STORAGE SPACE.

All the Amenities

Accented with semiprecious stone tiles, this spacious bathroom is a gem of convenience and comfort.

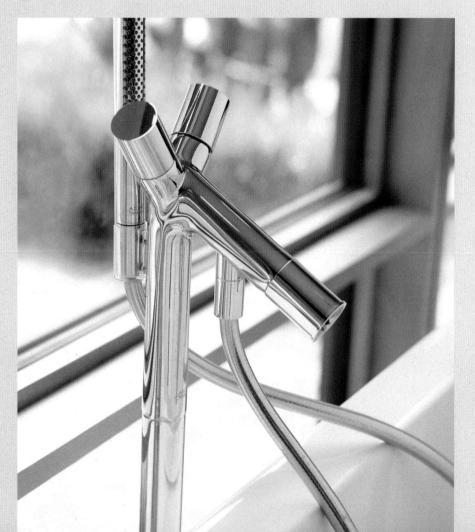

Left: A sleek tub filler reflects the overall style of this updated bath. Mounting the fixture on the floor plays up the sculptural quality of the tub.

Opposite: The horizontal windows framing the landscape are a hallmark of high-style ranch houses. Filling the wall from floor to ceiling and wrapping the corner, the windows bring light and views indoors.

289

Adjacent to an exercise room, the master bath features a large soaking tub, wall-hung sinks (the second one is on the wall opposite the one shown), and a urinal outside the toilet closet. Onyx tiles make a dramatic backdrop for the sinks.

When you think of tile for a bathroom, semiprecious stone is not what normally comes to mind. Onyx, a form of quartz with a wonderfully translucent quality, is more often associated with jewelry. Covering a wall in the bath with this colorful stone takes pampering to new heights.

Visions of the perfect bathroom can be influenced by gender. From a male point of view, the ideal bathroom may include a urinal. Unlike the ones found in public men's rooms, residential urinals can be pure sculptural forms hung on the wall of the ultimate gentleman's loo.

The view of the garden plays an important part in this home design, so the architect designed a cantilevered window that runs from floor to ceiling, embracing the outdoor scene. Thick hedges around the yard ensure privacy; a large, built-in window shade can be pulled down to block the view.

Left: The sleek, tubular lines of the wall sconces repeat the design of the tub filler and emphasize the contemporary sensibility of the room.

Below: This pivoting towel bar offers a practical solution for drying two towels.

Opposite: This wall-hung sink offers generous space on each side for grooming and toiletries, but visual clutter must be kept at a minimum in front of the highly patterned and decorative wall. A wallmount medicine cabinet hanging in the recess above provides ample storage space.

OPPOSITE: THIS CYLINDRICAL SEAT IS A
WHIMSICAL ALTERNATIVE TO A BUILT-IN
TILED BENCH. IT LOOKS MOVABLE BUT
IS ACTUALLY STATIONARY. COVERED IN
CUSTOM-MADE ¾-INCH TRAVERTINE
FLOOR TILES, IT HAS AN UPHOLSTERED
APPEARANCE.

ABOVE: THE ULTIMATE CONVENIENCE FOR A MAN,
THIS URINAL HANGS OUTSIDE THE SEPARATE SPACE
FOR THE TOILET, WHICH CAN BE CLOSED OFF WITH A
HIDDEN POCKET DOOR.

General Resources

To see the latest offerings in ceramic tile and natural stone, architects, interior designers, and builders attend Coverings, an international trade show held in the United States (the location changes annually). Architects and designers can bring one or two clients to the show. For more information, visit www. coverings.com or have your architect or designer contact NTP, Coverings Show Management, at 703/683-8500.

Note that product lines change regularly. Frequently cited sources of products shown in this book include the following:

Ann Sacks: 800/278-8453; visit annsacks. com to see the online catalog, find pricing information, and locate a showroom.

Dornbracht USA, Inc.: 800/774-1181; visit dornbracht.com to search for a retailer or showroom in your area.

Kohler: 800/456-4537; visit us.kohler.com for more information about products or to locate a dealer.

Walker Zanger: Visit walkerzanger.com to view the online catalog, find a list of authorized dealers and showrooms, and get contact information for your region.

Waterworks: 800/998-2284; waterworks.com.

In the source listings that follow, a (T) means that the product is available only through architects, interior designers, or other members of the trade.

Trends

Page 12: Jacuzzi towel-warming drawer. Photo courtesy of Jacuzzi Whirlpool Bath. Jacuzzi products are available through authorized dealers, showrooms, Lowe's Home Improvement Stores, and online stores. Visit jacuzzi.com for more information. To view details on the warming drawer, type "warming drawer" into the Product Search box.

Page 13: Integrated 24-inch indoor/outdoor warming oven from Dacor (IOWO24). Photo courtesy of Dacor. For more information or to locate a dealer, visit dacor.com.

Page 14: Séura illuminated mirror "Lola" in the Lumination Collection. Photo courtesy of Séura. Visit seura.com to learn more about the mirror and to locate a dealer.

Page 15: Séura Enhanced Series vanity television mirror with vanishing technology. Photo courtesy of Séura. Visit seura.com to learn more.

Page 16: Photo by Joshua Savage Gibson. Architect: Jim Strickland, Historical Concepts, historicalconcepts.com. Interior design: Ruth Edwards, Ruth Edwards Antiques and Interiors, Hilton Head Island, S.C. Millwork: Pinckney Brothers Construction, Hilton Head Island. Faucet: Kohler #K-6813-3 Georges IV Brass faucet with High Country spout and cross handles in polished brass.

Page 17: Photo by Gordon Beall. Designer: Robert Young. Cabinetry: quartersawn oak; hardware, Aged Bronze Knob #7034, Aged Bronze Pull #7035; cabinets with woven-wood door inserts: KraftMaid Cabinetry, 800/571-1990; kraftmaid.com. Leather tile backsplash: Cowden Bell Crosshatch Leather Tiles in Caramel for Ann Sacks. Sink: Kohler Iron/Tones #K6588 in Black'n Tan. Faucet: Ann Sacks Tate Lavatory Set #AS7005 in Weathered Copper. Countertop: DuPont Corian in Suede.

Page 18: Photo by Eric Roth. Design: Duffy Design Group, Boston.

Page 19: Photo by Eric Roth. Design: Horst Buchanan Architects, Cambridge, Mass.

Pages 20-21: Photo courtesy of Kohler Co. "Kathryn" console in Tea Green.

Pages 22-23: Photos courtesy of Philip Watts Design. Scoop sink (page 22) and Connect sink (page 23) are fabricated in solid cast resin and hand-finished in chalk white; also available in custom colors on request. For U.S. distribution of Philip Watts Design, contact Robert Rudd, Rudd & Associates; 678/445-5556; email: gracelighting@comcast.net. Philip Watts Design, Nottingham, Great Britain; email sales@philipwattsdesign.com. Visit the website at philipwattsdesign.com.

Pages 24-25: Photos courtesy of Linkasink. Smithsonian Collection, "Castle" (page 24) and "English Cutwork" (page 25). Visit linkasink.com or call 866/395-8377 to find the nearest showroom.

Pages 26-27: Photos courtesy of Alessi Spa.

Sinks, toilet, and bidet from the IlBagno Alessi Dot collection. To order Alessi products contact A F Supply, 22 West 21st St., New York, NY 10010; 800/366-2284. Visit alessi.com for more information about product lines.

Pages 28-29: Photos courtesy of Kohler Co. "Karsten" two-piece toilet with dual force flushing (page 28). Purist "Hatbox" toilet (page 29).

Pages 30-31: Photos courtesy of Clark Sorensen. Nautilus and Pink and Green Orchid urinal are just two examples of Sorensen's original, handmade porcelain urinals. Visit clarkmade.com to see his functional sculptures and prices and to contact him about a purchase.

Pages 32-33: Photos courtesy of Philip Watts Design. "Gloo-Illuminating" is designed for commercial spaces but can work in residential ones too. Molded in medium-density polyethylene with embedded LED lighting, the fixture glows with your choice of six colors. "Red Spoon" is an award-winning design, handcast in solid resin. "Pale Ale" is made of pressed galvanized steel set on a plinth that may be built from oak, walnut, laminates, stainless steel, or solid surfacing. See under Pages 22-23 for contact information.

Pages 34-35: Photos courtesy of Steuler Tile. Available to the trade through Valde Flooring, the exclusive distributor of Steuler tile in the U.S. Contact at 25 Denton Ave., New Hyde Park, NY; 516/326-3555. Email at info@ valdeflooring.com or visit valdeflooring.com.

Pages 36-37: Photos courtesy of Kohler Co. Sok overflowing bath for two with effervescence and chromatherapy (page 36) and Purist bath whirlpool (page 37).

Elements

Page 40: Photo by Eric Roth.

Page 41: Photo by Sam Gray. Interior design: Gauthier Stacy, Inc., 112 Shawmut Ave., 6th Floor, Boston, MA 02118; 617/422-0001; gauthierstacy.com

Pages 42–43: Photo by Sam Gray. Interior design: Mark Christofi Interior Design, Inc.,

348 Park St., Suite 106, North Reading, MA 01864; 978/664-8354; christofiinteriors.com.

Pages 44-45: Photo by Eric Roth. Interior design: Gayle Mandle Interiors, Providence, R.I.

Page 46: Photo by Emily Minton-Redfield. Architects: Scott Lindenau and Elish Warlop, Studio B Architects. Tile for walls, floor: Ann Sacks. Tub (#0446480000) and sinks (#0447530000): Duravit USA; 888/387-2848; duravit.us. Faucet for sink: Vola Collection, through Hastings Tile and Bath Collection; 800/351-0038; hastingstilebath.com. Mirror-mounted luminaries: Artemide "Robbia Half," Farmingdale, N.Y.; 631/694-9292; artemide.us. Cabinetry design: Studio B Architects, Aspen, Colorado; 970/920-9428.

Page 47: Photo courtesy of Ann Sacks. Barbara Barry "Glamour" mirrored vanity by Kallista for Ann Sacks.

Pages 48-49: Photo by Eric Roth. Design: Siemasko + Verbridge Architects, Beverly, Mass.

Page 50: Photo by Eric Roth. Design by Gregor Cann Design, Calif.

Page 51: Photo by Eric Roth. Interior design: Mary Wellman Associates; marywellmanassociates.com. Architect: Albert, Righter & Tittmann Architects, Inc., Boston; alriti.com.

Page 52: Photo by Michael Garland. Interior design: Doug Dolezal, Miller/Dolezal Design Group, Rancho Santa Fe, Calif. Wall paint: Benjamin Moore "Hepplewhite Ivory"; 888/236-6667; benjaminmoore.com. Sinks: Kohler Co. "Memoirs." Lighting: Wroolie & Co. "Normandie" faceted two-light sconce; wroolie.com (T).

Page 53: Photo by Eric Roth.

Page 54: Photo by Eric Roth courtesy of Trikeenan Tileworks. Design: Kristin Powers. Shower floor tiled in Elemental 1×1-inch grid in Random Whites. Walls in 3x6-inch brickbond and all trim in Milk White. Shaving rail tiled in Classic Highland crown. Ceiling is tiled in Elemental 1×1-inch grid. Visit trikeenan.com or call (603) 355-2961 to locate

a showroom. If you're in New Hampshire, visit the retail showroom in Keene, where overstock and seconds are also available.

Page 55: Photo by Colleen Duffley. Interior design: Amy Howard, Amy Howard Collection, Memphis, Tenn.; 901/547-1448. Architect: Mike Sullivan, Looney Ricks Kiss, Memphis. Walls: Venetian plaster. Flooring: Carrara marble. Ottoman ("Ram's Head"), vanity, étagère: The Amy Howard Collection (T). Ottoman fabric: Stroheim & Romann "Trenton Egingle Texture"/Oatmeal #8666N-0038; 718/706-7000 (T). Chandelier, window treatment (antique sliding doors): owner's collection. Tub: custom. Art: by Rana Rochat through David Lusk Gallery; 901/767-3800.

Pages 56–57: Photo by Eric Roth. Design: Heather G. Wells Architectural Interiors, Boston/Chicago.

Page 58: Photo by Maura McEvoy.

Page 59: Photo courtesy of Ann Sacks. Barbara Barry "Glamour" bath/whirllpool by Kallista for Ann Sacks.

Pages 60-61: Photo by Eric Roth.

Page 62: Photo by Tria Giovan. Design consultants: Phillip Hunter and Sim Harvey, Arcanum Antiques and Interiors, Savannah. Wallcovering: Waterhouse Wallhangings, Chelsea, Mass. (T). Tub: Ultra Baths; 800/463-2187; ultrabaths.com. Netting around tub: Pier 1 Imports; 800/245-4595; pier1.com. Mirrors: Waterworks. Sinks: Kohler Co. Sink faucets: Dornbracht USA, Inc. Sconces: Circa Lighting, Savannah; 912/447-1008.

Page 63: Photo by Gordon Beall. Interior design: Barry Dixon, Barry Dixon Inc., Warrenton, Va. Tub conversion: Baths From The Past; bathsfromthepast.com. Shower curtain, window shades: custom; Agora Interiors, Inc., Alexandria, Va.; 703/823-7800. Tile: Renaissance Tile & Bath, Inc.; rentile.com. Wall sconces: 20th Century Lighting, Inc.; 20thcenturylighting.com.

Pages 64-65: Photo by Eric Roth. Design: S+H Construction, Boston.

Page 66: Photo by Andreas von Einsiedel. Design: Claudia von Auersperg, London;

claudiaauersperg.com

Page 67: Photo by Susan Gilmore. Architect: Kurt Baum, KBA Architects, Deephaven, Minn. Tub: Philippe Starck for Duravit; duravit.com. Tub faucet: Porsche Design, available through Minnesota Standard Showplace; 952/920-1460; spscompanies.com. Art: Luis Gonzales Palma, Weinstein Gallery, Minneapolis. Walls: Venetian plaster by Otto Painting Design; 952/474-2022.

Page 68: Photo courtesy of Kohler Co. Spa Tower by Eric Cohler.

Page 69: Photo by Michael Weschler Photography. Interior design: Geoffrey DeSousa. Project manager: Gabriela Horikawa, De Sousa Hughes, San Francisco, Calif.; 415/626-6883; desousahughes.com. Fixtures, faucets, vanity mirrors, towel racks, towels, soaps, tile: Waterworks. Floor, architectural trim: Fox Marble & Granite; 415/671-1149. Mirror, shower surround: Paige Glass Co.; 415/621-5266.

Page 70: Photo by Eric Roth courtesy of Trikeenan Tileworks. Design: Kristin Powers. Lower wall in Sharkskin 4x4-inch tile with Classic Highland crown used as a base cove. Classic Highland rails and cornices in Bamboo framing 3-inch hexagons in Sand Grain and Sharkskin. Floor tiled in 1×1-inch grid in Random Bamboo Blend. Ceiling is 1×1-inch grid in Sharkskin. Visit trikeenan.com; see under Page 54.

Page 71: Photo by Eric Roth, courtesy of Trikeenan Tileworks. Design: Todd Tsiang. Shower walls tiled in Elemental LFB staggerbond pattern installed vertically, all in Vermont Green. Visit trikeenan.com; see under Page 54.

Page 73: Photo by Michael Partenio. Interior design: Brian Gluckstein and Stephen Wagg, Gluckstein Design Planning, Inc., Toronto. Mirrored desk: Elte, Toronto; 416/785-7885. Lamps on desk: Brunschwig & Fils Wilshire Lamps; 800/538-1880; brunschwig.com (T). Chair with slipcover, custom painting: through Gluckstein Design Planning, Inc.; glucksteindesign.com.

Page 75: Photo by Edmund Barr. Cabinets: KraftMaid Cabinetry, Dresden Maple Cabinets, Frost glaze finish; kraftmaid.com. Sink: Kohler

Co. #K-2241-8-96 "Memoirs" Lavatory, biscuit; #K-13132-3A-BN "Pinstripe" Lavatory Faucet, brushed nickel. Mirror: Aero #1382-2 Estate Mirror. Light fixtures: #W559 Pendleton, brushed nickel; #W880 Three Forks, brushed nickel; both with #156CE shades from Rejuvenation. Rug: Dash & Albert Rug Co. #RDA015 Siena rug.

Page 77: Photo by Marty Baldwin and Jay Wilde. "Eva" vanity from Oly; visit olystudio.com for the nearest retailer. Chippendale side chair: Chairs International, chairsint.com. Drapery: The Silk Trading Co.; 800/745-5302; silktrading.com. Silver bamboo picture frame: Pottery Barn (product line varies). Leather mat on vanity, wood container, shawl, makeup: Target Stores (product line varies).

Page 78: Photo by Marty Baldwin and Jay Wilde. "Julia" writing desk, "Rose" oval mirror, "Rose" chair from Swedish Blonde; 800/274-9096; swedishblonde.com.

Pages 80-81: Photos by Colleen Duffley. Dressing table: by La Barge from Maitland-Smith; 336/812-2400; maitland-smith.com. Chair: Hickory Chair, "Adam" side chair 5037-02 with chair fabric 2505-11; 800/349-4579; hickorychair.com. Tub: Waterworks "Cambridge" DUBT39. Lamp: Barbara Barry "Beaded Lamp" BBSO4TS through Baker; 800/592-2537. Fabric shade: "Rheims" from Shayam Ahuja; 011 91 22 24 926017, shyamahuja@vsnl.com.

Page 82: Photo by Kevin Lein. Interior design: Charlotte Moss. Dressing table: early 19th century chinois dressing table, skirt made of raw silk trimmed with embroidery from a Chinese robe. Dress on mannequin made from antique sari fabric.

Page 83: Photo by Gordon Beall. Interior design: Robert Young. Side chair: McGuire Furniture Co., Laura Kirar Dining Ring Side Chair/Slate #M-282; chair fabric "Headlands Collection Chenille"/Osetra #PHCH817. Countertop: DuPont Corian in Suede. Leather tile panel on back wall under counter: Cowden Bell Crosshatch Leather Tiles in Caramel for Ann Sacks. Area rug: "Walt"/Endive, Designer's Reserve Collection: Tufenkian Artisan Carpets.

Powder Rooms

Page 86: Photo by Nicholas Ruel. Design: Elise Brault, Gladwyne, Pa.

Page 87: Photo by Emily Minton-Redfield. Interior design: Dan Carithers. Wall upholstery: Brunschwig & Fils "Nicobar Cotton Print"/Blue #71189-222 by Gaston y Daniela; 800/538-1880 (T). Wall sconces: bronze appliqué from Travis Antiques & Interiors; 404/233-7207 (T). Mirror over vanity: antique, Italian, from Jacqueline Adams Antiques & Interiors; 404/355-8123. Vanity base: granite columns.

Page 88: Photo by Andreas von Einsiedel. Design: Rodrigo de Azambuja, Lisbon.

Page 89: Photo by Emily Minton-Redfield. Interior design: June Price, K.L. McCall Interiors Ltd., Atlanta; 404/364-0628. Mirror: custom, Brooks & Black; 404/365-0067. Wallpaper: Lee Jofa "Panelwork" #EY2041/Taupe, red square by Warner of London; 888/533-5632; leejofa.com (T). Countertop: by Stone Improvements Corp. through K.L. McCall Interiors. Faucet ("Royale" wallmount 2-hole faucet/Weathered Brass #HTW003004-70) and vessel sink ("Vista"/Botticino #RENSKVISTABOTT-70, 18-inch drop-in bowl): Renaissance Tile & Bath Inc.; 800/275-1822. Cabinetry: custom, K.L. McCall Interiors Ltd.

Page 90: Photo by Eric Roth. Design: Gayle Mandle Interiors, Providence, R. I.

Page 91: Photo by Michael Weschler Photography. Design: Mark Christofi Interior Design, Inc., 348 Park St., Suite 106, North Reading, MA 01864; 978/664-8354; christofiinteriors.com.

Page 92: Photo by Sam Gray. Design: Gauthier Stacy, Inc., 112 Shawmut Ave., 6th Floor, Boston, MA 02118; 617/422-0001; gauthierstacy.com.

Page 93: Photo by Eric Roth. Design: Weena + Spook Interiors; weenaandspook@aol.com.

Page 94: Photo by Gordon Beall. Architects: David Estreich and Brian Blackburn, David Estreich Architects, New York City; 212/463-0500; davidestreich.com. Interior designer: Gail Green, Green & Co., Inc., New York City; 212/541-3728; greenandcompanydesign.com.

Sink: Porcher; 800/359-3261; porcher-us.com. Gold faucets, towel rack: Dornbracht USA. Toilet: Toto USA; 800/350-8686; totousa.com. Round mirror: Mirror Brot, available through Design Bath & Hardware Inc.; 310/358-9669 (T). Walls: marble.

Page 95: Photo by Michael Garland. Regional editor: Robin Tucker. Interior design: David Dalton, David Dalton Inc., 1084 S. Fairfax, Los Angeles, CA 90019; 323/525-3155. Vanity and countertop, sink, glass tiles: Ann Sacks. Faucet, sconces, towel ring: Ginger, 888/469-6511. gingerco.com.

Pages 96–97: Photos by Jamie Hadley. Interior design: Wendy Owen Isbrandtsen, Wendy Owen Design, 6015 Grove St., Sonoma, CA 95476; 707/933-0881 or 415/717-3845 (cell); wendyowendesign@mac.com.

Traditional Appeal

Pages 100–103: Photos by Fran Brennan. Interior design: Marjorie Carter, ASID, Dublin, N. H. Decorative painting: Segreto, Inc., Houston; 713/461-5210; segretofinishes.com. Wallpaper: Waverly; waverly.com (product line varies).

Pages 104–109: Photos by Gordon Beall. Interior design: Irwin Weiner, ASID, Irwin Weiner Interiors, Ltd., New York City; irwinweinerinteriors.com. Mosaic floor: Studium, New York City; 212/486-1811; custom design by Irwin Weiner. Cabinetry: Exquisite Custom Cabinets, Norfolk, Va. Cabinet hardware: Sherle Wagner, sherlewagner.com. Fixtures and faucets: Davis & Warshow, New York City; 212/593-0435. Shower doors: Binswanger Glass, Virginia Beach, Va.; 757/425-9227. Towel warmers: Waterworks. Antiqued mirror panels: Mirror Fair, New York City; 212/288-5050. Window drapery fabric: Zoffany; 800/395-8760; zoffany.com. Window trim fabric: Scalamandre; scalamandre.com (T). Antique ceiling pendants: David Duncan Antiques, New York City; 212/688-0793. Sconces: Urban Archaeology, New York City; urbanarchaeology.com. Venetian mirror: vintage, Venice to Paris, Ltd., New York City. Decorative painting: Joel Souza, Virginia Beach; 757/620-3261. Bench: Lewis Mittman; lewismittman.com (T); with upholstery fabric from Nancy Corzine (T).

Pages 110–115: Photos by Eric Roth. Design: Heidi Pribell, heidipribell.com.

Pages 116–121: Photos by Joshua Savage Gibson. Architect: Richard Skinner & Associates Architects, Jacksonville, Fla.; 904/387-6710; rs-architects.com. Interior design: Terry Schneider, T. Schneider Interior Design, Jacksonville. Flooring, Calcutta Gold marble mosaic: Waterworks. Vanities and millwork: Neena Corbin, CKD, Morales Construction, Jacksonville. Fixtures and faucets: Kohler #K-700 tub and #6905-4 Georges IV brass faucet. Wall color: custom. Sconces: "Claudia" sconces in pewter from Ironware, Nashville, Tenn.; ironwareinternational.com. Wallpaper: Brunschwig & Fils, "Coutnay Strie" in aqua; brunschwig.com. Dressing table: Amy Howard collection; amyhowardcollection. com. Rug: Darren Jaffe Oriental Rug Gallery, Jacksonville. Chairs: "Eugenie" by Rose Tarlow for Melrose House, Los Angeles; rosetarlow. com (T). Chandelier: "Biarritz," Niermann Weeks; niermannweeks.com (T).

Pages 122, 125: Photos by David Duncan Livingston, davidduncanlivingston.com. Design: Martha Angus and Susan Wicks, Martha Angus LLC, San Francisco; 415/931-8060. Stone flooring: Jerusalem Gold limestone, Fox Marble, San Francisco; 415/671-1149. Fixtures and faucets, wainscoting tile: Waterworks. Border tile in floor: Country Floors, Inc., San Francisco; 415/241-0500; countryfloors.com. Wall covering: Donghia Furniture/Textiles, Ltd.; 800/366-4442; donghia. com (T). Hanging lantern: Niermann Weeks; niermannweeks.com (T). Ottoman fabric: Nobilis, Kneedler-Fauchere, San Francisco; 415/861-1011. Decorative painting: Katherine Jacobus, available through Martha Angus, LLC. Mirror and decorative box: C. Mariani Antiques and Restoration; 415/541-7868. Ottoman at dressing table: Martha Angus. Ottoman upholstery fabric: Fortuny, through Sloan Miyasato, San Francisco; 415/431-1465; sloanm.com.

Pages 123, 124: Photos by Matthew Millman. See under Pages 122, 125 for resources.

Pages 126–129: Photos by Tria Giovan. Interior design: Larry Laslo, Larry Laslo Designs, New York City; 212/734-3824. Black wall sconces: Baccarat, designed by Philippe Starck; baccarat.fr. Marble wall and floor tile ("Calacata Luna"), border ("Paradigm"/Hourglass White), ceiling molding ("Paradigm Rietvelt Molding"/Flannel), base molding ("Paradigm Bauhaus base"/Flannel), washstand ("Calacata" stone and "Paradigm" washstands), washstand base (oil-rubbed bronze): Walker Zanger. Mirrors: "Kentshire" mirrors, Walker Zanger. Sink faucets ("Octopus on Shell faucet"): John Landrum Bryant; 212/935-0999. Toilet: Kohler "Hatbox" toilet. Tub: Neptune "Zen," neptuneb.com. Bath faucets: Tradition Series from THG USA; thgusa.com. Available through Kraft Hardware; 212/838-2214. Giacometti-inspired Classic bench and Giacometti-inspired Sand Dollar chandelier in white resin by Carole Gratale Inc., through John Rosselli; 212/593-2060 (T). Vanity: Larry Laslo Designs for Directional. Art: by Andre Villers through Karl Kemp & Assoc. Ltd. Antiques; 212/254-1877. Trim paint: Benjamin Moore "Atrium White"; benjaminmoore.com.

Pages 130–133: Photos by Jamie Hadley. Interior design: Wright Stewart, Jones Design Studio, San Rafael, Calif. 415/454-8091. Marble floor and tiles: Walker Zanger. Sinks: Kallista; kallista.com. Faucets, tub, hardware, sconces: Waterworks. Chair, bench: Oly Studio, Berkeley, Calif; olystudio.com.

Pages 134–141: Photos by Gustav Schmiege. Regional editor: Susan Fox. Interior design: Julia Blailock, Blailock Design; 5120 Woodway Drive, Houston, TX 77056; 713/622-8005. Wall finishes: Leslie Sinclair, Segreto Inc., 10211 Memorial Drive, Houston, TX 77024; 713/461-5210; segretofinishes.com. Custom cabinetry: Memorial Builders, Houston, 713/266-6500. Iron and wood candelabras in art niches: Ceylon & Cie, 1319 Dragon St., Dallas, TX 75207; 214/742-7632. Italian sconces flanking mirrors: Jill Brown, 2940 Ferndale St., Houston, TX 77098; 713/522-2151. Oushak area rug ("his" area): Creative Flooring, 2410 Bissonnet St., Houston, TX 77005; 713/522-1181. Indian area rug in room center and to tub: Stark Carpets, 5120 Woodway, Houston, TX 77056; 713/623-4034; starkcarpets.com. Oriental rug ("her" area): Krispen, 3723 Westeimer Rd., Houston, TX 77027; 713/621-4404. Sink and fixtures: polished nickel and traditional country spout, Rohl; rohlhome. com; 800/777-9762. Oval air tub: Bain Ultra; bainultra.com; 800/463-2187. Iron tripod table near tub: Baker; 800/592-2537; kohlerinteriors. com. Winter Cloud marble on countertops: Walker Zanger (regional showroom, 7055 Old Katy Rd., Houston, TX 77024; 713/880-8999); walkerzanger.com. Honed travertine tiles, crema marfil mosaics and Sicis Zinnia glass mosaics on floor: Materials Marketing, 3433 W. Alabama, Houston, TX 77027; 713/960-8601. Seeded glass doors in towel cabinet: Dauphin Sales, 8556 Katy Freeway, Houston, TX 77024; 713/522-3418. Antique doors: 19th-century Italian, Watkins Culver, 2308 Bissonnet, Houston, TX 77005; 713/529-0597.

Glamour

Pages 144–149: Photos by Deborah Whitlaw-Llewellyn. Interior design: Shon Parker, Shon Parker Design, Atlanta. Architects: Bill Harrison, AIA, Dawn Bennett, AIA, Harrison Design Associates, Atlanta; harrisondesignassociates.com. Tub, vanities, faucets, shower fixtures, floor tiles, sconces: Waterworks. Wall paint: Sherwin Williams "Relaxed Khaki" SW6149; trim and ceiling paint "French Ivory" SW8017 from the Martha Stewart Collection; sherwin-williams.com. Round mirrors: Bungalow Classic, Atlanta. All fabrics: Duralee; duralee.com (T). Chandelier: through Shon Parker Design.

Pages 150–155: Photos by Gordon Beall. Interior design: Barry Dixon, Barry Dixon Inc., Warrenton, Va.; 540/341-8501; barrydixon.com. Bath designer: Lois Kennedy, CKD, Portfolio Kitchens, Vienna, Va.; portfoliokitchens.com. Wall finishes: Warnock Studios, Washington, D.C. Garden urn sinks: Istrian Floor Urn #213, Renaissance Stone; 800/456-7123. Concrete tub base: Concrete Jungle, Inc., Frederick, Md.; concretejungleonline.com. Tile: tumbled Botticino from Renaissance Tile & Bath, Alexandria, Va.; 703/549-7806.

Pages 156–161: Photos by Jeff McNamara. Bath design: Annie Kearney, manager, Tile and Stone Dept., Klaff's of Danbury, Danbury, Conn.; klaffs.com. Tile and stone design: Jayne Mason Fitzgibbons, Klaff's of Danbury. Bath fixtures design: Lisa Natale-Contreras, Klaff's of Danbury. Interior design: Robin McGarry, ASID, Robin McGarry & Associates, Weston, Conn; robinmcgarry.com. Countertops and wall tile: Calcutta Gold marble. Floor tile: Jerusalem Bone limestone. Shower mosaic and mosaic border: Bardiglio marble. Shower hardware: Harrington Brassworks Victorian-style thermostatic shower valve with Klaff's hand shower on bar. Shower nozzle: Perrin & Rowe 8-inch rain head with Klaff's eight-jet showerhead arm and flange in nickel finish. Sink faucets: Harrington Brassworks cross-handle lavatory. Sinks: Toto undermount white sinks. All available through Klaff's.

Pages 162–171: Photos by Michael Garland. Field editor: Robin Tucker. Interior design: David Dalton, David Dalton Inc., 1084 S. Fairfax, Los Angeles, CA 90019; 323/525-3155. Wallcovering: Phillip Jeffries, Ltd.; 800/576-5455; phillipjeffries.com. Floor: "Seagrass," Walker Zanger. Ottoman and vanities: custom designs by David Dalton Furnishings; daviddaltoninc.com. Vanity hardware: Liz's Antique Hardware, 453 S. La Brea Ave., Los Angeles, CA 90036; 323/939-4403; lahardware.com. Sinks: Kohler. Tub and sink fixtures: Ann Sacks. Tile behind tub: Ann Sacks. Whirlpool tub: Hydro Systems Co., 3798 Roundbottom Rd., Cincinnati, OH 45244; 513/271-8800; hydrosystems.com.

Pages 172–175: Photos by Tria Giovan. Architect: Louise Brooks, Gullans & Brooks Associates, New Canaan, Conn.; gullansandbrooks.com. Interior design: David Kleinburg Design Associates, New York City. Bathroom designer: Euro Antique Services, Inc., Brooklyn. Floor: crema marfil marble, black granite cabochon available through Felix Lorenzoni Studio, Inc., Greenwich, Conn.; 203/531-6050. Vanities and tub surround: Euro Antique Services; 718/349-8083. Tub faucet and hand shower: Waterworks. Sconces: Holly Hunt, Chicago; hollyhunt.com.

Pages 176–179: Photos by Tria Giovan. Interior design: Bellacasa Design Associates, Inc., The Woodlands, Texas; bellacasadesign.com. Cabinetry color: Sherwin Williams #SW 1124 Old Color; sherwin-williams.com. Sconces: Restoration Hardware; restorationhardware.com. Chandelier: Currey & Co. Fabric on window seat cushion: GP&J Baker; 516/752-7600. Dressing table and chair: Barbara Barry for Baker Furniture; bakerfurniture.com.

Pages 180–187: Photos by Ed Gohlich. Field editor: Andrea Caughey. Interior design: Sy John Iverson, Inside Story, 1480 Broadway, #2525, San Diego, CA 92101. Stone floor

and counters: "Kalahari red" marble. Sinks: Porcher; porcher-us.com. Bench: Genghis Khan; gkfurniture.com. Drapery fabric and hardware: Romo, romofabrics.com. Wall paint: Bayside Paint; baysidepaint.com. Sink faucets: Rohl; 800/777-9762; rohlhome.com. Tub: Hydrosystems Inc.; hydrosystems.com. Mahogany moldings: Mission Molding; missionmolding.com. Accessories: Bed, Bath & Beyond, Pier 1 Imports, Cost Plus World Market; Designer Gallery, San Diego.

Pages 188–193: Photos by Andreas von Einsiedel. Interior design: Graham Viney, Graham Viney Design, Cape Town, South Africa. Email: graham@viney.co.za. Chaise, chaise fabric (toweling), sconces (Morocco), Buddha head, vanity sink and faucets, vanity skirt (antique veil): owner's collection. Mosaic floor, walls, shower: Mosaik, 011 44 20 7795 6253 (London).

New Country Style

Pages 196–199: Photos by Michael Garland. Field editor: Robin Tucker. Interior design: David Dalton, David Dalton Inc., 1084 S. Fairfax, Los Angeles, CA 90019; 323/525-3155. Flooring: ebonized white oak, custom finish. Vanity: Berbere World Imports Inc., Culver City, CA 90232; 310/842-3842; berbereimports.com. Vanity top: honed fossilstone, Stone Mart, 13425 Sherman Way, North Hollywood, CA 91605; 818/299-9810; stonemart.com. Sinks: Kohler. Sink fixtures, towel rings: Newport Brass, a division of Brasstech, Santa Ana, Calif. 949/417-5207; brasstech.com. Sconces: Bluegrass Home, through Visual Comfort & Co., 7808 Kempwood St., Houston, TX 77055; 713/686-5999; visualcomfort.com (T). Mirrors, shelf unit: custom, David Dalton Furniture. Shower fixtures, tub fixtures: Perrin & Rowe, presented by Rohl; 800/777-9762; rohlhome.com. Steam shower: Mr. Steam; mrsteam.com. Tile: custom, "Sunflower." Window shades: Brambila Draperies, 5012-20 W. Venice Blvd., Los Angeles, CA 90019; 323/939-8312.

Pages 200–207: Photos by James Carrier. Interior design: Wendy Owen Isbrandtsen, Wendy Owen Design, Sonoma, Calif.; (see under Pages 96–97). Wallmounted sink faucets: weathered copper, from Newport Brass, a division of Brasstech, Santa Ana, Calif.

949/417-5207; brasstech.com. Shower fixtures: oil-rubbed bronze, Santec., Inc.; 800/284-4050; santecfaucet.com. Tub, tin mirrors, mesquite ottoman with French quilt upholstery, vintage linen draperies and rods, antique stone pavers, antique accessories: Wendy Owen Design.

Pages 208–215: Photos by Michael Partenio. Residential design: Dennis Kyte, Dennis Kyte, Inc.; email dykte@snet.net. Tub fittings and wall sconces (Easton collection), hand shower, levers, towel hooks, towel bars, sink faucets (Etoile collection), tub with whirlpool (Cambridge collection), sinks (Crystal-Leg Wash Stand from the Boulevard collection), shaving mirror at sink (Crystal collection): Waterworks. Chandelier: French antique, from Michael Trapp, Inc., Cornwall, Conn.; 860/672-6098. Black and white urns flanking window: Ettore Sottsass, homeowner's collection.

Pages 216–219: Photos by Michael Partenio. Tub, sinks, mirrors, lights, border tiles, shower, fixtures, wall tiles, floor tile: Waterworks. Chairs: custom design.

Pages 220–223: Photos by John Reed Forsman. Interior design: Greg Walsh, Walsh Design Group, Minneapolis. Tub: Architectural Antiques, Minneapolis; archantiques.com. Wallpaper: no longer available. Tub spout, handheld shower: Sunrise Specialty Co.; sunrisespecialty.com. Wallmount mirror: Gatco, Inc.; gatco-inc.com (T). Bathroom door hardware: Schlage Lock Co.; schlagelock.com. Holder for soap and cups: Restoration Hardware; restorationhardware.com (product line varies). Light fixtures flanking mirror: Rejuvenation; rejuvenation.com. Sink: St. Thomas Creations, National City, Calif.; stthomascreations.com. Sink faucets: Phylrich International; phylrich.com. Three-tier storage unit: Palecek; palecek.com.

Pages 224–227: Photos by Dave Henderson. Interior design: Nancy Serafini, Boston.

Pages 228–231: Photos by Carter Berg. Columns: Midnight Farm, midnightfarm.net.

Pages 232–235: Photos by Jamie Hadley. Interior design: Wendy Owen Isbrandtsen, Wendy Owen Design, Sonoma (see under Pages 96–97).

Pages 236–241: Photos by Michael Garland.

Design: Butterbrodt Design Associates, Del Mar, Calif.; 858/792-5400. Cabinetry: Evanko Cabinetry, Inc.; 619/441-0114. Faucets: Samuel Heath & Sons, New York City; samuel-heath.com. Sink/tub: Kohler. Windows: Pella; pella.com. Cabinet hardware: Alno Inc., Chatsworth, Calif.; alnoinc.com. Shower: Perrin & Rowe by Rohl; 800/777-9762; rohlhome.com. Tile: Walker Zanger. Venetian mirrors: homeowner's collection. Window shades: F. Schumacher and Co.; fschumacher.com (T). Chandelier: Dennis & Leen, West Hollywood, Calif.; 310/652-0855.

Contemporary

Pages 244–249: Photos by John Granen. Interior design: Norman Lloyd and Gabor Kalman. Fixtures: Lavabo Agape Spoon tub and Block sink; giant.co.uk. Faucets: Dornbracht "Tara" tub faucet and "Meta" sink faucet. Floor and walls: Cobra slate. Shower floor and walls: Brazilian slate. Wallpaper: Cannon/Bullock Robin Mulberry paper; cannonbullock.com. Cabinets: Mike Danielson, Blu Collar, Seattle; 206/501-5884.

Pages 250–255: Photos by James Carrier. Architect: Steve Rankin, Steve Rankin Architecture, Oakland, Calif.; 510/653-2534. Decorative artist: Lynne Rutter, Lynne Rutter Murals and Decorative Painting, San Francisco; 415/282-8820; lynnerutter.com. Cabinetry: City Cabinetmakers, San Francisco; citycabinetmakers.com. Tub hardware: Waterworks #ARCL7236. Sinks: Vitraform "Round Frosted Undermount," vitraform.com. Faucets: Vola; vola.com. Shower hardware: Dornbracht USA "Tara." Pendants: Translite Sonoma "Varnish"; translitesonoma.com. Sconces: Artemide "Dulcet," Farmingdale, N. Y.; artemide.com.

Pages 256–259: Photos by Janet Mesic-Mackie. Architect: Thomas Meyer, FAIA, MS&R Architects, Ltd., Minneapolis; msrltd.com. Interior design: Jodi Gillespie, ASID, MS&R Architects, Ltd. Medicine cabinet: custom, Woodshop of Avon, Inc., Edina, Minn.; thewoodshopofavon.com. Sink bowls: American Standard; americanstandard-us.com. Faucets: Chicago Faucets, Des Plaines, Ill.; chicagofaucets.com. Glass soap bowl: Redlurered, Minneapolis; redlurererd.com.

Pages 260–265: Photos by Gordon Beall. Design: Robert Young. Design consultants:

Janice Pattee, CKD, CMG, Janice Pattee Design; Robert Kuo, Robert Kuo Design. Lanai tub/whirlpool (Onzen Soaking Tub/Eight-Jetted Whirlpool #AS4936-Jet) and faucets ("One" deck mount bath set #AS6426, Charcoal): Ann Sacks. Soaking tub/whirlpool surround: DuPont Corian solid surface in Serene Sage. Antique carved door panel: Robert Kuo. Siding paint: Benjamin Moore "Texas Leather" #AC-3. Wall surfaces (Corian in Sagebrush) and floor surfaces (Corian in Concrete): DuPont Corian. Master bath tub (Robert Kuo Copper Repousse Zen Bath #AS9119), tub faucet ("Tate" exposed floor mount bath set #AS6040 in Weathered Copper), sinks (Robert Kuo Copper Repousse Zen Basin #AS6101), sink faucets ("Tate" wall mount lavatory set #AS5570 Weathered Copper), mirrors (Robert Kuo Copper Repousse Tessa Mirror #AS9121), tile (Erin Adams custom art glass "Organic Complex Basketweave" mosaic tile mural): Ann Sacks. Countertops (Corian solid surface in Concrete), walls above sinks (Corian in Sagebrush): DuPont Corian. Sconces flanking mirrors: Christian Liagre "Arthur Sconces" #HCO-SCN in Noir Patina, Holly Hunt; hollyhunt.com.

Pages 266–269: Photos by Jeff McNamara. Interior design: Gail Green, Green & Company Inc., Interior Designers, New York; 212/541-3728. Mosaic floor and wall tile (Erin Adams); leather tile, accessories, hardware, mirrors (by York Street Studio), lavatories (Orlo); water closet (Kallista); plumbing hardware (One): Ann Sacks. Light fixtures: Jean Karajian Gallery; 212/751-6728. Medicine cabinet and accessories: Dornbracht USA. Lucite and leather bench: York Street Studio; 800/967-5401. Shower partition: Varia Collection by 3 Form; 800/726-0126.

Pages 270—273: Photos by Ed Gohlich. Field editor: Andrea Caughey. Interior design: Evi Avinante, ASID, CID, Avinante & Associates, Inc., Interior Design/Architectural Color, San Diego, Calif.; eviavi@mac.com. Architect: W. Dean Meredith, AIA Architect, P.O. 2142, Del Mar, CA 92014; 858/755-5591; ArchitectDeanMeredith.com. Walls: redwood and ocean green slate. Countertops and flooring under tub: teak. Door surround: Honduras mahogany. Tub: cedar, Oregon Hinoki Products; originalhinokiproducts.com. Sink, fixtures: oil-rubbed bronze, Rocky Mountain Hardware; rockymountainhardware.com. Lighting: through Evi Avinante.

Pages 274–279: Photos by Ed Gohlich. Field editor: Andrea Caughey. Interior design: M. Megan Bryan Studio, 7661 Girard Ave., La Jolla, CA 92037; 858/551-2622. Floor, shower tile: Modern Builders Supply; modernbuilderssupply.com. Glass slider (toilet compartment): J.J. Scoots. Tub: Diamond Spas Inc., 760 S. 104th St., Broomfield, CO 80020; 303/665-8303; diamondspas.com. Fixtures, sink, shower: Lefroy Brooks, XO series; lefroybrooks.com. Vanity: light wood, Japanese sen; dark wood, Japanese sen stained. Cabinetry fabrication: Design Synthesis, San Diego; 858/271-8480; designsynthesis.net.

Pages 280–283: Photos by Janet Mesic-Mackie. Residential design: Ralph Hoffman, MAP Lab, Inc., Chicago; maplab.com. Interior designer: Chris Garrett, Garrett Paschen Ltd., Interior Design and Decoration, Evanston, Ill.; garrettpaschen.com. Floor tile: Ann Sacks Linen limestone. Vanity and cabinetry: Ralph Hoffman; 312/432-0870. Fiber laminate: Abet Laminati; abetlaminati.com. Fixtures: Dornbracht USA "Tara" series. Hardware: "Mackintosh," Horton Brasses, Inc.; horton-brasses.com. Sconce: Kozo Lighting #S14, satin-nickel finish; kozolighting.com.

Pages 284–287: Photos by Quentin Bacon. Architect: Cole Harris Associates, Westport, Conn.; 203/226-1830. Sinks and tubs: Kohler Purist line. Tub faucet: Kohler Laminar.

Pages 288–295: Photos by Kim Golding. Field editor: Leigh Elmore. Architect: Paul Minto, Urban Prairie Architectural Collaborative, P.C., 4436 Fairmont, Kansas City, MO 64112; 816/304-7416. Tub: oval with panel and support frame #700012 by Philippe Starck for Duravit; duravit.com/products (T). Wallmount sink and siphon cover: Starck 3 Washbasin by Philippe Starck for Duravit (T). Sink faucet: "Axor Starck Classic Lav Mixer" in polished chrome by Hansgrohe, hansgrohe-usa.com (T). Shower fixtures, tub faucet, hand shower: "Axor" in polished chrome, Hansgrohe. Shower tile: Travertine custom cut, beige, through Luxe Home, Chicago Merchandise Mart, Kinzie & Wells (T). Urinal: #803036 by Philippe Starck for Duravit. Wallmount light fixture: "Kubit" in polished chrome by Ginger; gingerco.com. Wall tile: onyx in green and red.

Enjoy Your Home

*make it everything you've **dreamed***